Rhetorical Candy

KJ Hannah Greenberg
With Rivka Gross

Seashell Books
www.myseashellbooks.com

Acknowledgements:

Hannah is grateful to Michael Greenberg, her husband, without whom her life would be incomplete. Rivka is grateful to all of the men (big and small) in her life who have taught her more than any book ever could.

Table of Content

1. The Morality of Israel

2. The Sanctity of Israel

3. The Social Milieu of Israel

4. Worldly Reactions to Israel

Preface:

Most goings-on can be interpreted in at least two ways, only one of which usually gets proffered. It makes no difference what the topic is or which perspective gets favored; folk generally stick to a single position. Consider the subject of The Modern State of Israel. Few among the globe's population are Israelis. Nonetheless, the majority of the world's denizens vociferously disagree amongst themselves on: the morality of Israel, the sanctity of Israel, the social milieu of Israel, and appropriate responses to the existence of Israel.

Leaders and followers, alike, would be well served to learn more about the Holy Land, especially more about: nationalism versus universalism, the character and function of democracy, and the essence of diplomacy. To boot, politicos educated in the traditions of the west, specifically, and other world citizens, more generally, would gain from increasing their understanding of: freedom of speech, economics, the philosophy of science, Zionism, and Judaism.

The State of Israel is an amazing place, well-deserving of informed discourse. This country's fruit crowns world agricultural, the Holy Land's high tech is second to none, and her military know-how, too, is superlative. Most importantly, Israel *is* this globe's spiritual capitol. There's a lot for mankind to learn about and from Israel.

Toward that end, the sixty-two narratives that constitute *Rhetorical Candy* reflect on images of, suppositions about, and lived experiences indigenous to Israel, including: Asian laborers, rebbes toting BUL M5-pistols, and five year-olds chaperoning three year-old siblings, via public transportation, to school. This book's graphic writing style additionally captures: sunsets over Jerusalem, traditions woven into local celebrations of life events, and the awesomeness of the Israeli medical system.

The Jewish state is neither an ongoing beach party nor a perpetual war zone. Rather, Israel is a place of great supernal energy as well as home to egrets, hyraxes, and other extraordinary samples of Creation. All of us lose when Israel is misunderstood. We need books like *Rhetorical Candy* to correct erroneous portrayals of this nation. We need to taste truth about Israel, if only one essay at a time.

Dr. KJ Hannah Greenberg
Jerusalem, 2018

Introduction: All Things Blue and Green

I used to harbor affection for all things blue and green. My world was one of ultramarine and cobalt, of viridian and cerulean. After making aliyah, I developed a new aesthetic. Now, umbers and siennas, cadmiums and ochres stir me. Where once woodlands and carpet-like valleys moved me to develop free verse or to reach for literal canvas, these days, sandy hilltops and burnt-looking wadis provoke me to write and to paint.

It is difficult to know whether I consciously changed to acclimate to my external surroundings or whether my external surroundings, without invitation from me, caused my metamorphosis. I dreamed of living in The Holy Land, but never thought that my desire would become actualized in my lifetime. I was a secular academic whose vision had been limited to two children and to tenure at some state university.

Fortunately, life can best our fantasies. I was blessed with four children, abandoned academia, and found myself on a religious journey. I was, however, ill-prepared for the ways in which life in Israel would differ from life in The New World. The changes I have been undergoing, ever since switching geographies, sometimes make me feel alienated, and often bring me to otherworldly ends. There has been great disparity between my Old World and my New World experiences.

Consider that this land's innate holiness prejudices my comprehension of sensate information (it is dubious that any logic can account for the difference between my dancing in a forest one day, making Aliyah overnight, and then embracing a dry river bed the next day.) Not only are the literal (and, similarly, the figurative) hues of this Old World's landscape different from the hues of my former home, but the textures and the gradations of clarity, of this setting, too, are distinct from my former life's textures and gradations.

In The New World, natural objects were smooth, in general, in no small part due to the amount of water generated from the sky and stored in the ground. In my previous domain, fieldstones were smooth, plants were smooth, and trees were smooth. Here, in contrast, fieldstones are ridged, plants are prickly, and trees, when they exist at all, too, are bristly (ponder New World maples and crabapples versus Old World acacias and jujubes.)

Also, in the Holy Land, every prayer for rain and dew is a sincere petition for life (versus what was, over there, sometimes, a mouthing of scripted words). This Old World's proximity to intense scenery makes me feel as if my "seat" has been moved from the balcony to a row front and center. In Israel, I am much better located than I was in North America to witness Creation.

Another visual difference between the two realities is in the boundaries among entities. In that other place, "actor" and "acted upon" were usually optically distinct. A house looked different than its inhabitants. Small mammals, and the ground from which they derived their sustenance, too, were dissimilar. Here, though, there is less perceivable dissimilarity. Here, a house looks sandy and its indwellers, too, look sandy. Small mammals look coarse, and the ground from which they sustain themselves, too, looks coarse. In Israel, the visual limits blur.

Sight is not the only sense that diverges between here than there. Sound, smell, taste, and touch, equally, yield contrasts between my former and current worlds. Consider the neighborhood women whom gently push my cart, at the local butcher shop, while I am steering it, and who mutter, in Hebrew, all the while, some soft sentiment about time and want. In my other place, very few socially normal people would transverse someone else's personal space to adjust a shared environment.

In North America, as well, few socially normal people articulate their needs; over there, verbal camouflage substitutes for social variation. Here, in contrast, local ethnics mutter in ancient tongues while bagging shoppers' selections. Local shoppers, if sufficiently perturbed, add to the ensuing cacophony by articulating their opinions until a shop noises with a world's worth of languages.

Other auditory differences between here and there include bird sound.

Over there, I was privy to morning-time tweets and peeps. Over here, in this city of hills, in which I live near the top of one prominence, not aviary voicifications, but aviary wing songs, make themselves known (around my home, it is mostly lizards that chirp.) That type of conspicuous whistle, moreso, differs among species. "The sound of raven" is unlike "the sound of pigeon." Plus, all birds' wing sounds are especially powerful when they are diving from the heights above our apartment to the valley below. Avian mating advertisements, though not unique to the Land of Israel, like most things, are amplified here.

It is not only what I see and I hear, in this Old World, that sends new information to my brain; my other senses, too, give me unfamiliar signals. I have grown accustomed, for instance, to alliums. My friends' hugs are spiced by leeks, my children exhale garlic while they chatter, and my neighborhood's air, especially before Shabbat and holidays, is filled with the pungent smell of onion. If uncooked hot peppers had a detectable scent, I imagine that they, too, would be part of the local tang.

Whereas capsicum does not always influence the wind, it does impact cuisine. When I was a graduate student living in international university housing, I failed to comprehend my peers' penchant for things piquant. As an Israeli, though, I cannot imagine a day without some version of "hot sauce." Despite the fact that the produce here has a measurable intensity, most of us residents slaver all manner of strong condiments onto our comestibles.

Touch, too, is more powerful in Israel than elsewhere. Although nettle and rosemary also grow in moister regions, the indigenous pharmacopeia is bold in the degree to which its plants' stems and leaves feature mostly hair and scales. From *Artemisia* to the lavenders, in vacant lots, on roadsides, and on balcony container gardens, the texture of sun-deflecting botanical mechanisms is exaggeratedly pronounced.

Similarly, stones, in Israel, are not merely solid aggregates of minerals that are capable of reflecting ambient temperatures, but are palpable pieces of a greater topography. Individual bits of rock, here, are crucial environmental indicators, not waste. They are also primitive, physical indicators of meteorological futures.

It is not enough that my Israeli impression of Creation differs from my New World one because my senses now ricochet off of astonishing things. I must also accept that my post-sensory and pre-sensory ways of making meaning have changed here, in this unreal place.

Examples of the former include the ways in which my awareness of balance and of physical association has altered. Examples of the latter include my newly burgeoning intuition and my other forms of nascent "instinctive" knowing. Given this location's energetic conduit between people and Creation, my extraordinary senses, too, have influenced my concept of existence.

In the end, however, it does not matter if my altered comprehension comes through my "five senses" or by means of other intelligence. The Boss works this land in a way in which His fingerprint is more regularly perceptible than anywhere else. It ought not to surprise me that Israel is a more meaningful, more real venue than any other place in the world.

The Morality of Israel

Welcome Home

It a ceremony in Israel's main airport, my daughters giggled with a bunch of girls they knew from Jerusalem and from Chasmonaim. I spoke animatedly with friends from Bet Shemesh. Nearby, soldiers stood ready. To the other side of us, military men and women stood at attention. Next to them, a man with a long shofar saluted.

Little children held aloft signs that were larger than their heads. Tall grownups perched smaller children on their shoulders. In carriages, new sabras slept, oblivious. Some grownups were draped in blue and white. Others merely waved our flag. Israeli music made for a loud, upbeat background to announcements of incoming…

…olim chodeshim. Together, the pregnant, the parents of newborns, the grandparents, the children of all ages, sizes, and hashkafot, the middle-aged matrons and patrons, the singles, and others, waited, bounced, sung, and clapped as our collective rejoiced in the blessing of new Israelis.

Whereas many of the guests at this ceremony were natives, some were tourists, who gathered to welcome their families to the Holy Land, to where they, too, anticipated eventually settling. Sure, many of the guests were related to the new arrivals, but at least the same number was friends. Some hosts, in fact, had no one in particular to welcome; they had joined the party in order to greet other members of the Klal.

At the celebration, there were speakers from the organizing association, from the government, and from other significant places. The music of "Hatikva" brought tears to the faces of fluent Hebrew speakers and to the faces of those yet to enter the aleph level of ulpan. Beyond those sentiments, though, was the acknowledgment of the bravery of the individuals newly, officially entering Israel.

Suddenly the cheering grew louder. Shuttle bus by shuttle bus brought the pioneers who had just deboarded. Cameras whirred. Elders cried. Children climbed higher to get a view.

One hug at a time, one embrace of family, of friendship, and of Am Yisrael, at a time, one inhalation of the Old World at a time, the olim interwove with the locals. The sun ascended. Clock mechanisms continued to function. Flesh and blood, however, stayed fixed in an eternal moment.

Babies were hoisted by misty-eyed aunts. Strollers and carry-ons were lifted from the tired arms of travelers into the excited arms of their new neighbors. Israel's new citizens, the newest installment of our people's unending aspiration, were lauded. The olim were laden with well wishes…

…and with welcome signs, gifts, fruit baskets, candies, toys, and more. The newbies were feted with hot and cold refreshments, and with other "party favors." They were invited for Shabbat and sma'achot, and were asked whether or not their children needed the bathroom. Meanwhile, men hugged. Tiny girls, speaking several different languages, danced. All was good in the universe.

In the days to come, those new olim would deal with rental headaches and with schooling heartaches. They would seek work, make friends, and look for medical care. Most would cry, a few would wonder if they made the right choice, and a minuscule per cent would actually go back to bitter Diaspora.

Long after the signs had faded, the flags had tangled, and the pageantry had been relegated to memory, those men and women, their children, their parents, and the spirit of advancement, which they packed along with their suitcases, remained to fortify and to improve our precious nation since their handbags held more than a night's worth of disposable diapers or a week's supply of prescriptions. The new olim's carry-ons also contained the wisdom that Jews belong here, in Israel, and that Jews ought to stop at nothing to get here, to live as Am Yisrael in Eretz Yisrael.

In the newcomers' wallets was more than New World currency and various types of photo identification. In their wallets was also heart-creased sketches and love-filled poems, was reflections of gratitude concerning the chance to live the dream of our people and to do so in this lifetime.

Close to those new arrivals' central parts, beyond their Magen Davids and their miniature mezuzot, were their prayers, including that soft, yet strong, frequently unspoken sensibility that we await Moshiach and that our thoughts, our words, and our deeds must be part of our communal efforts to bring him home.

Consequently, new people gift us more established folk more than we gift them. They bring faith and trust. They restore our hope with each footstep that they take from the edge of their airplanes into the core of our nation. Their journey forges our shared future. We need them. We need every single oleh chodesh!

Welcome home!

A Bat Bayit's Aliyah

Sometimes, I don't mind living vicariously. When a much loved bat bayit made aliyah, I felt no compunction when experiencing joy and gratitude through her transformation. In fact, I was grateful to part of her estimable journey.

Before I was able to feel my most recent rush of gratitude, however, I had to deal with pragmatics. Specifically, Missy Younger and I woke up at dark to catch a ride to the center of town, from where we took a Nefesh bNnefesh-sponsored hasa'ah to Ben Gurion Airport. We packed potato chips for Missy Younger and goat yoghurt for me, a *Sefer Tehillim* and a siddur, welcome signs for our new olah, and the few items that our beloved immigrant had requested we bring along.

Baruch Hashem, because my family had merited knowing many of that year's new citizens, even the cab driver, whom we called before five in the morning, was familiar with our routine; cab to city center, hasa'ah to airport, hasa'ah back to Jerusalem and then local buses to school and to home. When he picked us up, he didn't ask where we were going, but how many olim we were meeting.

That chilly morning, Missy Younger and I were thankful that our hasa'ah had already arrived in Jerusalem. We boarded and snuggled, alternating between snatching bits of sleep and being inspired by the new sky, which Hashem was tinting as we rode toward the airport.

At the correct time, we said "Tefillah Haderech." Thereafter, throughout most of the rest of the trip, we were charmed by the seminary girls who sat directly behind us. Those young ladies spoke softly to each other about many matters, including their health and the Holy Land's Shemittah observance.

At last, we arrived at the terminal where guests could greet the newcomers. In addition to us pedestrian sorts, there were politicians, IDF officials, and other individuals of social standing. There were members of the press, soldiers, and more than one musician, too. The soldiers' presence was especially meaningful to our loved one, as she had often told us that she felt that the young enlisteds best represent the country she was adopting.

Other aspects of the tempo of Israel were apparent in the terminal, also. In some corners, tallit-clad men called "shacharit, shacharit." In others, young people marked their faces with blue crayon, sketching Hebrew words and Magen Davids onto their skin. In yet others, people were sipping hot beverages. Above that humanity were pasted, on the terminal's walls, giant montages of photos taken of olim arriving in The Holy Land. Around those guests, the music of our nation played. Those Hebrew melodies ranged from "Shalom Aleynu" to "Machar," and later to "Hatikva."

Suddenly, a coterie of seminary girls, distinct from the ones who had sat behind us on the bus, ran into the hall. They wore, on their shirts, words of welcome in Hebrew and in English and claimed a section of the floor for their lively dances. Their enthusiasm buzzed the crowd.

Other comers hoisted their signs, practicing for the olim's landing. Homemade, heartfelt greetings sprouted on various canvases, in various media, with various shades of the same intent; all of us were glad to be in a situation in which we were already of the land and in which we were empowered to welcome our loved ones home.

In short time, we were given the cue to go outside to greet the shuttles bringing the new arrivals from their plane. As one, we took pictures, waved placards, and cried.

With deserved pomp, the new olim made their way through the aisle formed by the soldiers. From infants, exhaustedly asleep in their buggies, to grand matrons wheeled forward into their new lives, the immigrants burst upon us.

There were enough hugs, smiles, and tears for everyone. Suitcases switched hands since the established folk were eager to provide any small comfort to the new ones. Thereafter, the hosts ran to furnish sandwiches, to point out bathrooms, to provide cell phones, or to otherwise yield tenderness. Tired olim slumped in appreciation around their friends and family.

Our own loved one borrowed a cell phone to make a special call. Once the connection was established, she began her conversation.

"Mom?" she offered.

There was a pause, likely a mirrored greeting from across the world.

Then our loved one added those incredulous words; "I'm here!"

It's so easy to get bogged in the coarser aspects of survival in this land. It is so easy to become occupied with financial, health, and personal growth issues. However, during sacred moments, such as when a new olah speaks words that encapsulate the experience common to all of us, we are reminded why we dwell in Eretz Yisrael.

I remember once witnessing one friend give another mussar. The first woman had complained about other Jews with differing religious habits. The second woman had responded by pointing, from the Kotel Courtyard, where all of us were standing, to the Temple Mound and to the alien structure that she hoped, very soon, would disappear from there. "Achdut, not assessment," that wiser other had whispered. That sagacious ima had cooed in Hebrew, a second language for all of us, yet her words were as honeyed as the land which we are settling. Simply, Hebrew is holy. Because it is holy, Hebrew is powerful.

It was with much gratitude that my family welcomed our Bat Bayit to Israel. However, we welcomed her in English. At her Ben Gurion Airport ceremony, English was everywhere. English was the language of most of the speeches, English was the language printed on at least half of the signs, and English was the lingua chosen by most of the guests.

Even though most of the greeters seemed a click or two different from most of the new arrivals, the former's Israeliness having seeped into their stances, proxemics, and dress, those more established Holy Land, dwellers, nonetheless, spoke the language of their birth nations. In fact, not only did those more established Israelis speak English, but they also adjusted their personal space per North American norms, gestured like individuals from South Africa or Australia, punctuated their talk with pitch and pace more closely resembling that of Brits than of indigent Israelis, and interspersed their speech with snippets of French, Yiddish, and Russian.

Those sounds and gesticulations seemed odd to me, a resident of a predominantly Israeli neighborhood, where the main language remains Hebrew. While I felt comfortable with my ability to comprehend the Anglo mannerisms swirling around me, I felt out of sorts with the lack of local language. Most of the newbies knew Ivrit, so in some ways the use of so much English made no sense. Maybe there was a comfort factor involved.

When my family lived in the States and visited immigrants from Russia, we heard Russian at the Shabbat table. When we had Shabbat with people from Switzerland, German was spoken intermittent with English, and so on. I think that the deficit of Hebrew at the reception was due to a combination of fatigue, joy, and habit.

I believe, as well, that notwithstanding the languages that the new olim spoke when they landed and notwithstanding what they will speak in the future, the vast majority of them, especially given the helpful agencies available to them, especially Nefesh bNefesh, who chartered their flight, and given the klita offices in Israel's major cities, and more, will quickly and easily find their "Israeliness." The Internet has made cultural fluency trouble-free. From online language lessons, to articles about living in Israel, to Judaic chat rooms, and more, olim today can begin their acculturation long before they arrive. Baruch Hashem!

At the airport, our Bat Bayit was being treated like a queen. She had a reporter and a cameraman following her around from the time she processed her papers in New York, through her hours on the flight, and continuing through to her arrival at Ben Gurion. In addition, a friend of our Bat Bayit, whose first year aliyah anniversary coincided with our Bat

Bayit's flight, decked our loved one with a tinsel lei, which was the colors of the Israeli flag. Plus, the members of our family who could not join us at the airport called in to extend their greetings to our Bat Bayit.
Missy Older called from Tzfat, where Missy Older's class was performing chesed. Computer Cowboy called on route to a business meeting in Haifa. Older Dude and Younger Dude mumbled greetings from Jerusalem.

Two days later, during Shabbat in our home, the celebration continued. Our children, who had known this special young lady for years in the States, had no trouble returning her to her role as their adopted older sibling. Missy Older called again, before Shabbat, to wish our not so long lost "adopted" daughter "welcome home." Bat Bayit and Missy Younger, along with Murphy-the-Kitten, shared a room. Bat Bayit and Younger Dude exchanged a year's worth of missed taunts and jests. In addition, Younger Dude introduced our Bat Bayit as an Olah Chodesha to our other Shabbat guests and helped me talk, in Hebrew, to a rabbi in our minyon, whom, in turn addressed our minyon's gabai, who then announced, after services, but before everyone had dispersed, that our kehila had a chance to welcome a freshly minted Israeli.

After the second meal of Shabbat, a close family friend, who had met Bat Bayit during Bat Bayit's pilot year here, came over to share a hug. Later that afternoon, before and after my favorite Shabbat shiur, the shiur's regular attendees focused their motherly and grandmotherly attention on Bat Bayit. After Shabbat, Computer Cowboy took Bat Bayit to a local tzedeket for a bracha.

Motzi Shabbat, reinforced with extra blankets and with phone numbers of mutual friends, Bat Bayit made her way into her new Israeli life. We filled her with love. We filled her with joy. We hope we filled her with an appreciation for things Israeli. We're glad she's here!

Not so Exotic, After All

I am still growing. Specifically, certain ideas that today, in this Old World, seem obvious, were, not too long ago, in that New World, foreign, odd, and even alien. It was not so much that formerly I had limited knowledge of things charif or that I used to be clueless about the sorts of bridges that ought to be built among Jews, as much as it was that I was insulated from the realities of the Holy Land. While living in the States, I ate spicy food and welcomed all types of kippot to my home.

Nonetheless, after making aliyah, I experienced a reckoning. Expressly, when Computer Cowboy and I merited celebrating the return, to Israel, of a rabbi from our former town's va'ad, from its community council of rabbis, I experienced a paradigm shift.

We were excited about that reunion. The fellow being honored is steeped in Torah (may he and his wife live to 120, knowing only health and happiness), as well as is a leader who uses, b'ayin tova, his Torah wisdom to help his constituents with the practical bits and pieces of life. That principal member of our former kehila had assisted our aliyah by giving our family a simple, but vital directive. He pointed out which neighborhood we should live in when we relocated to the Old World. Without his guidance, our choice could have been nothing but foolish.

Before moving to Jerusalem, my family was ignorant about most of the Holy City's neighborhoods, specifically, and about the demographics of communities in Israel, in general. Like many aspiring olim, Computer Cowboy and I had researched possible places to root, via Israeli organizations' websites and by via lists provided by New World olim agencies. Nonetheless, our "informed" choices, in hindsight, could have been disastrous for our family.

The longer we live in Jerusalem, b'ayin tova, the more grateful we have been for this rabbi's advice. Today, we grasp why our new friends welcomed us with cautious surprise; without the rabbi's help, like most other newcomers, we would have remained oblivious to the existence of our wonderful, tourist trap-free, community.

At present, such realizations are "so many camels from an earlier caravan." What matters is the kindness that was freely and graciously given to us by the New World rav, who shepherded us. He is not the rav of our former shul. He looks a bit different from my family and he follows a minhag that is not our own. In fact, we only made this rabbi's acquaintance because we were trying to help with a community project that he held dear.

Regardless, while we still lived in the New World, that spiritual guide seemed exotic. He had lived in several countries, was championing a house of worship where "foreigners" gathered together, and spoke the languages of far-off lands. In short, we had never before met anyone like him. That was then.

At the luncheon, in contrast, this scholar seemed more Anglo than not, more American than Eastern, and hip to all sorts of things my family seems to be forgetting. While that rabbi's roots remain international and while his children study in both the East and the West, that Man of Torah is probably more comfortable than me, at this point, addressing Americans (my history of teaching public speaking notwithstanding).

Ironically, it is my family, not his, who has grown estranged from gefilte fish and averse to fancy sma'achot. It is my loved ones, not his, who have morphed into dwellers more ready to embrace scampering lizards than feral cats. My husband, my children, and I, not the exalted members of that rabbi's family, stick out among New Worlders. That precious rabbi continues steadfast among his congregants. We, on the other hand, have substantially morphed.

When Computer Cowboy and I said our good-byes to that incredible teacher, we nodded to each other in silent understanding. Our former advisor is not to be so exotic after all. He's less of a foreigner that we will ever be. May Hashem Grant him and his family a speedy aliyah!

Tzedakah: The Magnitude of a Proper Standpoint

Sometimes, we get too bent out of shape about material goods. I make this claim not from an apex of wealth, but from a position somewhere south of the financial equator. Specifically, fiscal well-being is not equivalent to affluence.

In fact, any equation, which makes wealth equal to prosperity, is false, at best. We Jews are meant to enjoy "success," in its various manifestations, but have never been promised that success would find us rolling in literal riches. Our treasures are not worldly goods in the same sense that our values are not worldly values.

We People of The Book, above and beyond all else, esteem living and learning Torah. Our principled direction affects not only our ways and means of worship, but also the ways and means by which we process the mundanities of our lives, including: which foods we eat, which clothes we wear, and the manner in which we build our homes.

I recall, once, in a ceramics workshop, hearing an administrator give over her opinion on how children should be handled. That day, I think I shrunk further than the clay. The ideas, which that woman espoused, were more about external reward and less about inner truth. In contrast, we, who live in Torah circles, walk the path of trying to please The Boss. Later, if at all, we might concern ourselves with each other's opinions. Among us, no laurels are awarded for behaviors whose aim is to increase individuals' popularity.

We know that we were not supposed to be focused on manipulation, but on the power of bringing our attention to our experiences. We consider ourselves successful when we remain responsive to The Big Guy.

Accordingly, when we give charity, we engage in such acts not to impress, but to bestow, not to gain recognition, but to ease others' burdens, not to compensate for our character flaws, but to develop our character strengths. Sure, our fortunes, and our sharing, thereof, might have their roots in tacit items like real estate, stocks, bonds, and other types of capital. Our assets, though, *have to* consist of compassion, sensitivity, and truth.

Our most important possessions, the only ones which we will bring with us beyond this realm, are the deposits we make through our deeds of loving kindness. Only those holdings will carry over to the World to Come.

The Importance of Hands on Giving

As a people, we have established needs. One of those needs is to share our resources. Such behavior is still, however, easier said than done. Consider the following, fairly sad tale.

On a sidewalk abutting a busy thoroughfare in Jerusalem, a man with sores, swellings, and other forms of visible suffering extended a cup that was partially full of coins. Next to him was a woman aged by a type of sickness known only to her and to our Creator. She, too, held out a miserably filled vessel.

Many people walked by that couple. Most of those pedestrians made no eye contact with the man or with the woman; perhaps the ordinary folk found it easier to be suddenly preoccupied than to acknowledge that the beggars are part of our family.

Infrequently, one or more passersby stopped to give the pair a kind word or some money. Interestingly, the donors seemed to be of a type; almost all of them were a little more unkempt, a little less fancy, a little less put together than were the mobs of humanity that walked by without stopping. To a one, the donors were of the ilk that is unafraid to be "sullied" by someone else's misfortune.

Interestingly, the donors were united not by their level of religiosity, since both the population that passed and the population that helped seemed to have equal per cents of black hats, knit kippot, and uncovered heads. Rather, the donors' commonality seemed to be their need to view other people as members of our Klal, as persons experiencing situations that, has v'shalom, could as easily have been our own.

The donors didn't need to know if the pair with their hands out were angels, were survivors of the Shoah, were mentally challenged, or were "merely" physically ill. The donors seemed only to care that they were able to provide a small amount of comfort to indigents and that they were able to acknowledge those persons' humanity.

I witnessed the generous souls' and the passersby's behaviors from inside of a sandwich store. I had ordered a bottle of juice, a bottle of water, and a bagel.

Later, besides coins, I gave each of the two sufferers an identical copy of the lunch I had bought for myself. Yet, our experiences still differed since I had been able to eat my meal in the relative comfort of the restaurant whereas the impecunious had to eat their food on the street (only in hindsight had I realized that I could have invited them inside to eat with me.)

Even after my nearly inconsequential sharing of money and food, I remained bothered by the fact that the majority of people who passed by the couple ignored or disdained them. Seeking solace, I went back to the restaurant to ask its moshgiach why so few people helped that particular set of unfortunates.

Regrettably, the learned man answered me with some technical rhetoric about when we Jews are obliged to give ten per cent of our holdings and when we are obliged to offer more. His response failed to satisfy me.

I'm not a tourist, a student, or any other type of temporary visitor to Israel. While I know less about life here than do many folk, I know enough about living, in general, to be convinced that it is rudimentary for all of us to help each other, and to act, with immediacy. I also know that even if I were a visitor, I would still be obliged to help where I could.

All of us have had "bad days." Our challenges come in the forms of health, of income, of marriage, of children, and so forth. We are powerless to impact the timing and severity of our tests. We are powerful only in how we cope with our ordeals.

For that reason, it behooves us not to judge, but to aid. While it is impossible to know why someone else is suffering, it is imperative that we extend a hand, a coin, or a smile to the needy individuals who have been placed on our lives' sidewalks.

Coming Prepared

Unfortunate situations exist. Sometimes, we feel overwhelmed by the number and kind of requests made for us to share our resources. We can cope by being proactive in our sharing. Specifically, it is to our advantage to plan to give away some of our worldly treasure before we encounter people in trouble.

Whereas it is meritorious to dedicate part of our earnings and part of our time to the needs of others, in general, it is also beneficial for us to dedicate part of the room in our suitcases to Israel's poor, specifically. Granted, we are required to fund disadvantaged members of our families before funding disadvantages members of our communities, but it is also the case that we are required to support Israel's troubled people.

Besides mailing checks across the ocean, we can bring our wealth with us to the Holy Land. Specifically, when we travel, rather than only packing goodies for loved ones, we can also pack goodies for Israel's poor.

It is nice to bring late model suits to this special country for our children learning in yeshivot or in seminaries. It is even nicer to employ suitcase space to bring a few used suits "home" for fixed income elders. Similarly, while it might be customary to port electronic devices for Israeli grandchildren, we'd be yet more elevated if we ported such gadgets for trauma victims.

We make sure to pack health aids for Israeli friends with discerning tastes. We can also make sure to pack health aids for Israel's medical organizations. When we bring tasty treats for former, New World neighbors, we can, equally, bring tasty treats for Israel's soup kitchens.

Because Israel is a geo-political island, goods cost most here than in many other places in the world. Similarly, since Israel is yet an emerging nation, wages are significantly smaller here than they are in Europe or in North America. Nonetheless, we often forget than a collection of eyeglasses, a box of pain reliever, or some outgrown children's clothes and shoes would be valued by many of Israel's citizens.

Let's try to leave space in our luggage for our brethren. Maybe we could, by design, pay for another suitcase so we could give this form of tzedakah. It's better to bring reading materials to Gush Katif refugees or to lug pacifiers for Jerusalem's infants than it is to pack a second coat or a third sweater. It's better to bring pencils for this nation's school children or towels for this nation's poor than to pack additional CDs or cosmetics.

If every visitor brought a few goods over, for the purpose of charity, each time he or she visited the Holy Land, there would be less suffering to witness. It is useful and necessary to support the portion of Am Yisrael that dwells here. Think about this type of charity, next time, before you pack up and fly over!

The Beauty of a Little Good

We Israelis aim high. The thresholds, to which we reach, whether determined for us by ourselves or by others, are not, ordinarily, low-hanging fruit. There's something about the nature of most individuals that makes us strive for the most meaningful "success" available to us.

Unfortunately, if we strive for significance because we seek external points of validation, our acts ill-suit us. Not only ought we not to judge ourselves or to judge other folk, but we especially ought not to allow others' assessment of us, in general, and of our intentions and achievements, more exactly, to guide our self-perceptions.

First, Hashem is the True Judge. Second, we fail in our Avodas Hashem, in our service to G-d, when we defer to human opinion. Sure, human beings, even those among us who have effectively and nearly completely escaped the urge to prove personal worth visa via social status, sometimes, still look outside to see how well we are doing. Consequently, the ends toward which we endeavor might, on occasion, be erroneous.

What's tragic in this equation is not our human fallibility. We've been designed to be imperfect, in part because such a lack inspires us to engage in mitzvot bein adom l'Makom, commandments governing the relationship between us and G-d, in part because suck a lack inspires us to engage in mitzvot adom l'chaveiro, commandments governing the relationship among human beings, and in part because such a lack leaves room for us to choose growth.

Rather, the heartrending quality of this verity, of this need for peer approval, is that we falsely suppose that by living in a down-to-earth manner we're living neither fashionably nor in a way that allows us to achieve high-minded ambitions. We're so wrong if we accept that falsehood.

Humility, per se, has never stopped being utilitarian. What's more, The Boss does see, does hear, and does record all of our goings-on. He knows and cares about all of our behaviors, including those we try, but do not satisfactorily complete.

Yet, we continue to embrace circumstances that "enable" us to avoid working through our dilemmas, i.e. to skip personal growth opportunities. Simply, as long as we adopt such outlooks, such as setting unrealistic aims, we disable ourselves.

For instance, per exercise, persons who are out of shape are best advised to begin with light dumbbells and short repetitions of exercises than with heavy weights and unmanageable numbers of repetitions of sets. Their immediate fitness goals, judiciously, need to be: strength, health, and learning how to be disciplined about exercise. Their ambitions ought not to include transforming themselves, magically, and mistakenly, into bulked up, or anorexic-looking individuals (in fact, such targets are harmful to everyone.) Revision takes time.

Correspondingly, those of us who are writers are well directed, especially as we move from nascent, namely, emerging careers to established ones, to seek humble, not choice, venues as our outlets and to invest our efforts into: integrating the elements of literature into our manuscripts, rewriting, rewriting some more, networking, using gracious communication, and learning how to receive rejections. Feelings of entitlement rarely bring anyone the same results as do hard work and an unassuming nature.

Comparably, first time parents benefit from seeking four consecutive hours of sleep per night and one hot meal per day. It's sad to see so many newbie moms and dads entangled in frustrations about imperfect parenting when their mood and attitude would improve if they had more sleep or better nutrition. Life events necessarily cause us to adjust our outlooks. If we can make peace with getting "only" some of our wants and needs met, no matter how mundane those ends might be, instead of kvetching about what isn't happening in our lives, our passages through trials will be less arduous.

In our more global interpersonal exchanges, too, when we manage to accomplish a small amount of good, we attain a great amount of virtue. It's invaluable if we cheer up, for half of an hour, a dear one faced with a marital crisis, if we babysit the kids of a friend juggling health challenges, or if, just for an afternoon, we process a few loads of laundry for a pal with an important career-building deadline. Unexceptional input can be extremely meaningful.

Likewise, when we offer to aid our children, students, or subordinates with tools, rather than with solutions, we are fashioning good results. Viz., teaching a person to fish is a much higher level of giving than is sticking a filet into his or her hand.

There are small acts of kindness, which we can direct toward ourselves, as well, that can make a big difference in the quality of our lives. We can gift ourselves with ten extra minutes of sleep one morning, a microwaved cup of tea rather than a cold glass of juice on another day, and an extra session of jogging on a third. It might behoove us, as well, even when we are not especially troubled, to decide to wear the nicer of two sweaters, to use one of the more expensive colognes in our collection, or to say a few extra passages of *Tehillim*. Too many folk save their shiny things for "someday," only to never enjoy them.

Whereas it might seem admirable to want to climb to great heights, and whereas others in our lives report to us that it's commendable for us to stretch as far as we can, attempts to exceed personal limits rob us both in the short term and in the long term. It's wise to take small steps since it's in regulating our purposes, not in meeting them, that we achieve sagacity. That said, our actions do not have to and, in fact, ought not to, be monumental.

Striving to Do Better

Sometimes, we not only relegate, but we actually lock away, in a place so distant from our affections that we can no longer tally our responses, our knowledge of other peoples' suffering. Generosity, that precious trait native to the realm of kindness, becomes hard to come by when we've lost the habit of being accountable for our brethren.

Recently, I received a widely broadcast email from a friend urging me to pray *Tehillim* on behalf of a small, seriously ill child, whom I do not know. Last week, I received an email from a friend in The New World asking me to bake challah on behalf of a barren kallah. Daily, my email box overflows with requests for funds from legitimate, Yiddishe nonprofit organizations.

Arguably, there seems to be no rift in our social fabric when seekers can approach, the rest of us without censure, whether they beseech electronically, via phone, or in person. On balance, all of us have finite time, money, and, sadly, willingness. Sure, we promise, three times daily, in the Shema, to serve Hashem with all of our heart, with all of our soul, and with all of our material well-being, but it is also true that we often forget, as the hours of our days and nights melt, that such service includes befriending members of the Klal.

Consider the story, told by a friend, of how, at a recent shiur, when perspective bocharim were visiting a yeshiva and the prayer hall was a few shtenders short, only one regular rushed to yield his own and then to scout through the school's closets for more furnishings. The other students didn't even think to budge.

Consider, as well, another case, in which an entire community looked the other way when confronted with the knowledge that a known child molester was hired to teach in their children's school. Although a few brave families relocated away from that neighborhood, in order to keep their most precious ones safe, other families minimalized the warnings by erroneously classifying them as hashon hara.

Our negligence need not be so profound. Sometimes, our specious focus can be one of feeling sorry for ourselves, or can be one of considering holiday preparation a burden, while forgetting, because of our self-pity, to call: the seminary girls, the elderly neighbor, the single bocher, or whomever else might not have a place for a seder, or might have a place, but might be feeling unnaturally lonely in the seasons of hustle and bustle (and blinders).

Even more minutely, one does not have to be a giant in interpersonal relations to remember to put the lid on the toothpaste, or to open the plastic rings that link beverage six packs (so birds won't later strangle on those rings). It does require an oversized sensitivity, though, to understand *and to want to* alter our actions such that other folk become part of our personal pictures.

Lifetimes are constituted by moments. In this moment, let's choose: to excuse a child for forgetting a chore, to encourage our fellows' Torah learning, to contribute to our synagogues' coffers, and to put out a bowl of water for the dumpster cats. Compassion can be the step by which we transcend mundanities. - Hannah

****

There is a story about a man who saw a boy walking on the beach. What drew the man's attention was not the fact that the boy was walking alone in the early morning on an otherwise deserted beach, but rather that the boy was bending over every few feet. As the man got closer, he was able to make out what the boy was doing; the boy was picking up stranded starfish and throwing them back into the ocean.

"You will never be able to throw all of them back in," said the man to the boy. "There are miles of beach and you are all alone. Anyhow, tomorrow, more starfish will get washed up. Why even bother?"

The boy looked at the starfish in his hand, threw it into the water, and then turned to the man. "You might be right," he began, "but it makes a difference to this one."

I wish I could say that I wrote that story. I didn't. I was, however, lucky enough to grow up with the knowledge that every small act of kindness matters. Nothing we do is for naught and even if others don't always appreciate our efforts, the recipients of those deeds, as well as Hashem, appreciate them.

I feel that in the world, kindness is not always practiced. It's certainly not always expected. When I was five, and walked three blocks to kindergarten, every day, I knew I could ask any stranger I saw along the way to "cross me, please." People were happy to take a minute to help a child cross the street.

Last year, though, I stood for at least half of an hour by the entrance to the open air market in Jerusalem and offered every older, woman, whom I saw, assistance with carrying their bags to the bus stop. Every single one was shocked that someone was offering to help them. All of them turned down my offer - no one makes the time to help anybody else any more.

I feel that this lack of compassion is wrong. Our technology has gone forward. Our interpersonal relationships need to move forward, too. In this crucial time of world oppression and of the birth pangs of Moshiach, nothing is more important that Ahavat Yisrael, loving your fellow Jew.

We Jews, as a nation, need to strive to stick together. Otherwise, we will fall apart. - Rivka

Judging Favorably

In this world of strum and drang, where rockets empty kindergartens, and where advertisers have found a way to employ Instagram to their benefit, it is especially worthwhile for us to be accountable for our individual behaviors. We are not off the hook, despite the many social goings-on that conspire to flood us, from maintaining proper civility.

"Proper civility," in turn, has many components, the most important of which is judging others favorably. Not only do we lack the wisdom to truly assess what is happening in the totality of the private or public lives of other people, but we ought not to want to make such assessments.

For me, that notion means, that if, for instance, one of my girls wants to wear makeup, even though I don't even lacquer my nails, she is not a bad seed. Rather, she is a bud seeking to healthfully differentiate herself from her gender-similar parent. She's going through her adolescent development in a constructive way.

Likewise, my son, who elected to attend a hesder yeshiva located at the border between the Holy Land and Lebanon, ought not to be considered a youth fleeing his familial sanctuary, but a youth running toward his religious destiny. That child, who holds dear the sanctity of life, would not hesitate to make the ultimate sacrifice to protect our land, has v'shalom it ever be necessary. Meanwhile, he'll continue to grow in good middot.

Similarly, another son, the one who sometimes sits quietly on our sofa during family meetings, the one who might be viewed, unfavorably, as a nonparticipant, is actually my family's most judicious member. That dear one measures his words. Often, he reminds the rest of us to stay on the derech by us not reacting too much or for too long to any good or bad news we receive. That son's emunah is enviable.

Additionally, my family's oldest child, fair of mind, while fruit-looped in humor, is not an upstart, but is a respectful young adult who cares enough to carefully point out that when families, ours included, move forward, they ought to do so without socially or psychologically sacrificing their children. Lucky will be the administration under whose auspices that daughter teaches when she finishes her degree.

My children were raised to be heedful of human nuance and to articulate their sentiments in keeping with that sensitivity. By being in touch with their feelings at the same time as being able to speak about them, my sons and daughters are empowered souls who ought to be respected and, maybe, emulated. They are not cheeky. They are not full of fluff. I need to look at them kindly and gratefully.

As per my husband, good 'ole Computer Cowboy, it is incumbent upon me, in my marriage, too, to see the good, and to believe, to truly deem, his objectives as beneficent, or, in the least, as neutral. For instance, when my man buys me flowers, it's better to think "how thoughtful," than "why not the yellow ones." When he surprises me and cooks the Shabbat soup, it's better to think "what a kindness" than "he forgot to use the leftover carrots." There's no reason why my partner of decades, b'ayin tova, would try to be anything but considerate in my direction.

What holds true for my family holds true for my other interpersonal exchanges, as well. Whereas a minority of folk cheats or otherwise misuses relational resources, most individuals do not think about and certainly do not actualize nasty behaviors. In short, if something in an interaction seems off, it's probably not personal, i.e. it is probably not outwardly directed, or is outwardly directed but is that way for reasons having nothing to do with me or any other second party.

For example, local drivers can be maddening, yet, it is vital for me to bestow the benefit of the doubt on each of them (while I simultaneously drive defensively). Some wheelers are actually rushing off to medical care. Some drivers are law enforcement agents chasing villains. Some roaders are persons scurrying to places of work such as banks or government offices, where the rest of us would be miffed if they, the staff, failed to show up. I'm not advocating hazardous driving; I am advocating compassion.

On checkout lines, too, empathy can be put into play. Maybe, the mom who scoots her cart in front of mine has a kid with a loaded diaper. Maybe, the fellow who reaches in front of me for the last package of low-priced packages of greens has a fixed income and a medical condition that require him to eat those foodstuffs daily, but to do so at a discount. The cashier who closes her counter just as I approach might need an impromptu bathroom break because she's pregnant.

Additionally, if a stranger takes my seats at shul, instead of inwardly ranting, I can praise G-d that another neshemah is joining mine for prayers. When someone litters in front of my home, instead of cursing their seeming thoughtlessness, I could notice the elderly person with whom they are walking. When someone dominates conversation at a simcha, instead of wrapping myself with resentment, I could appreciate that I don't have their chronic woes.

It's so much easier to frown at nail polish, to complain about a school's location, to feel aggrieved by a child that deliberately gives up his turns, or to silence a young adult who tries to point out blind spots, than it is to seek the good in other persons and to learn from the good that's already been found. Analogously, it is easier to curse "creative" drivers, to lament marketplace practices, and to laud moral supremacy over strangers than to see people as messengers meant to mirror my shortcomings.

Judging favorably is an important element of proper civility. It keeps people social and causes people improve themselves. If I strive to judge favorably, I'll add to society, and be a better person.

No Saintly Fools

Recently, I was informed, by another Israeli, that it's bad to be a "saintly fool." That remark, having been made by an adult, whom I esteem, confused me. I mulled over the rhetor's intent.

First, I had to distance my understanding of the denotative meaning of that phrase from its connotative meaning. Consider, for example, that Jews don't hold by "saints," per se. While we celebrate the admirable deeds of our forefathers, our kings, our prophets, and our "ordinary" learned leaders, and while we anticipate the footfall of Moshiach, unlike most other groups of people, we do not elevate persons above the mantle of "human."

Correspondingly, although in many places in our literature, we make fond reference to individuals who are "deficient" in judgment, we don't classify people as "sinners." Sometimes, people who make mistakes are lacking common sense, as exemplified by the residents in the Chelm stories. Other times, out literature's "foolish folk" are actually our wisest folk, are persons who wear rhetorical disguises so they can remain humble and hidden.

Thus, I struggled with the essential reference in my colleague's remark. I didn't know whether or not he meant that a "saintly fool" is someone who goes outside of conventions by dint of ignorance of those conventions, or whether or not he meant that a "saintly fool" is someone who strives to escape the rubrics of convention. Maybe my friend inferred something else, entirely.

I wondered, too, whether or not it is possible to be classified as possessing "saintly fool-like" qualities, by accident, or in other people's minds, but to not actually consider one's self to have those qualities. As well, "saintly fools" might be regarded as such but remain ignorant of that rubricking by their fellows. The epistemic implications of these many possibilities are numbing.

Fortunately for me, my fellow's remark was made within a context. I was led, by our talk, to believe that the demarcation "saintly fool" is good for cows or for ethnic cousins, but not for the likes of us. More specifically, our cultural norms, the sensibilities upon which we Jews base the gist of our words, despite protests to the contrary, are *not* the cultural norms of other religions.

Jewish axiological variables, i.e. values, are not necessarily the values of the outside world, except in instances in which our system of weighing thoughts, words, and deeds has been unconditionally and unequivocally adopted by other people, e.g. in the cases of personal freedoms, monotheism, and the like. Even in such circumstances, our ethics do not make meaning the same way in which the systems that have taken on our system do.

Specifically, Jew use laws, not rules, to understand human behavior. Laws derive from enforced sanctions, whereas rules tend to be grounded in need and tend to be adjustable to the demands of relationships. Contrariwise, our values are prescribed by Hashem in Torah. They are entirely nonnegotiable.

It follows that the sense we make out of social correctness or the lack thereof originates not in our desires, but in our responsibilities. Whether or not we *want* to govern, we are *obliged* to tithe (or, in these days, during which we await the rebuilding of The Temple, to tax) our income. We may *want* sagacious government officials to determine our people's course, but we *must* abide by their sometimes foolish decisions (except in such cases in which those decisions are in direct conflict with Torah).

If we deviate from our duties, then we are fools, for we give up some portion of our foreordained lives. Further, whether we separate ourselves from our standards through laissez faire attitudes or energized actions, the ultimate "rectification" to our wandering away from our rightful places is not any punishments meted out by our peers, but is any decree issued, for our sake, by Heaven. Other persons' poor choices must necessarily be immaterial to our own. We are required to act, not to react.

Simply, questions of functioning as "saintly fools," or not, are extratopical to Jewish life. Whereas we ought not to lapse into unnatural tolerance or even into imprudent means of constructing or maintaining our society, we also ought not to worry about whether or not we are looked upon, by other nations, as this side of crazy.

Consequently, the meaning I find myself assigning to my friend's caution is that we ought to avoid silly maneuvers. As well, we must not place ourselves in situations that push us to disavow our principles. We are commoners simultaneous with being the children of The King.

Pain

Recently, I lost a pregnancy. That loss, as was true for the pregnancy that preceded it, too, was for my good. It is as important for me to embrace and to celebrate the nullification of potential life, as it is for me to cry out in awe that Yours Truly, a woman of more than fifty years of age, b'ayin tova, received the grace of a "change-of-life" gestation.

In serving Hashem, we are supposed to be grateful for everything that happens to us, including and especially those aspects of our days and nights that we find difficult to incorporate or that we find upsetting to think about. Harm, heartbreak, trouble, and other "terrible" occurrences, in the end, are gifts, not punishments. Our work is to come to terms with the benevolence integral to those items.

Maybe such rigorous samples of Hashem's loving kindness are meant to route us away from our lesser manifestations of ourselves, i.e. to help us rectify our strayings. Maybe such harsh events are meant to pull us, our imperfections notwithstanding, to higher levels of actualizing ourselves, i.e. to help us approach, in the World to Come, heights closer to the throne of Hashem than we might otherwise have achieved. We can't and don't have to know why we go through any experienced anguish.

Likewise, we can't and don't have to erase any feelings we suffer in association with our growth opportunities. Psychic and physical injuries wound us. Loss hurts. The point is not to deny our reactions, but to concede them and then to give ourselves over to the goodness we derive therein.

Such a seemingly impossible stance is not unique to Torah living. The undergirdings of martial arts and the expressiveness of many creative endeavors, likewise, make clear this notion. Wisdom dictates that all of living is of a single piece and that the oneness of life is for our benefit.

Yet, we Jews do not agree to this view as a means to greater athleticism or as a means to make nicer paintings; we adopt this perspective because at its heart is Torah.

Rabbi Shalom Arush writes in "The Cow Comes, the Cow Goes," that "kapara [atonement] also means 'like a cow.' Whenever we lose something dear to us, we should always remember that Hashem is simply taking back a gift. We should never forget that everything in life is a free gift. Emunah is our only real comfort in this difficult world."[1]

Our afflictions, thus, on the one hand, are a vehicle for our joining together with HaKodesh Baruchu even when such hardship and misery extend past what we deem to be the measure of human capacity. It remains important for us to try to say "thank-you" for all that befalls us.

On the other hand, we continue to have no answers for why our people endured the Shoah (the Holocaust) or why: a friend's children are orphaned, a son's classmate is killed defending Eretz Yisrael, a dear one's husband remains unemployed, a beloved continues on as barren, an associate has lingering problems with in-laws, a neighbor's small daughter loses the classroom work she spent weeks preparing, or a stranger misses his bus. The workings of the cosmos defy logic.

In balance, all of us have heard stories of how: a broken car engine kept someone from vanishing in the death towers of 9/11, a co-congregant waited twenty years to meet her beshert only to be blessed with a man of great middot and a beautiful child, a teen was rejected at a certain Ulpanat in order for her to make great friends and to receive a wonderful education at a school she would not have otherwise considered, and a gift of home grown flowers, from an economically-challenged guest, became the most favored present given to a celebrant. Sometimes, behind the scenes benefits get revealed. Most often, though, they do not.

---

1. Rabbi Shalom Arush. "The Cow Comes, the Cow Goes." Trans. Rabbi Lazer Brody. *Breslev. co.il.* http://www.breslev.co.il/articlePrintVersion.aspx?id=24315&language=english.

Accordingly, it helps us when we admit that it feels impossible to be glad about "bad" things, i.e. that we struggle to accept that The Boss, gently or firmly, necessarily must leads us away from one manifestation of our lives to another. We even fail at trusting that Heaven's will is always for our good.

Rabbi Yehoshua Geller writes, "the Chazon Ish, in his sefer *Emunah Ubitachon, Faith and Trust*, Perek 2a, shows that bitachon [trust] is trust that everything that happens is from Hashem for the good or the bad. Everything is from Hashem. Period. Nowhere does it mention that we must always feel that all is for the best. Trust is about knowing that all is from Him whether we understand it or not."[2]

Quoting Rabbi Zeinvert ZT"L, Rabbi Geller continues, "I believe in the name of the Noam Elimelech, that Hashem wants us to not understand. It's not that we do not understand Hashem's ways. The not understanding is what He wants [Knowing is not the same as trusting.] Now the *Gemara* brings a story of Nachum ish Gamzu, who always said that all is for the best. This is a story of a [morally exceptional] Jew, who was famous for this trait. For the average person, the concept that 'all is for the good' is something for us to know now, but something we can only truly feel in the world to come."[3]

In other words, we can aspire to feel grateful for all of our agonies, but if we fall short, or if we are annoyed or worse with our encounters, those sentiments, too, are part of our development. What's more, it is our process of reaching for thankfulness, not necessarily only the gratitude, itself, that elevates us.

Rabbi Geller concludes, "we can always look around and see things that make it clear to us how Hashem made things for the good. We need to use those cases to strengthen us and to help us appreciate Hashem. Hence the pasuk, from *Psalms*, recited in "Ashrei," a prayer said thrice daily, 'ירבדו'

2. Rabbi Yehoshua Geller. Letter to the author. 5 Nov. 2014. TS.

3. Ibid.

החישא דיתואלפנ, I will tell of your wonder Hashem.' As we tell of wonders we see, it makes us stronger that the big picture we don't see also has an explanation."[4]

It follows that we live a life of faith by believing that everything is from Hashem and by believing that everything Hashem does is for our good. We're not required or able to understand causal relationships between our pain and our future (good) outcomes. We don't have to rise to the level of our perfectly righteous teacher Aaron, who was able to remain silent when his sons, Nadav and Avihu, were consumed by fire. Merely we need to stretch to grasp that Hashem's universe, without exception, is as it ought to be and that the universe's obligatory state is one of delight.

Rabbi Eli Popack observes, in a response to a question about Moshe consoling Aaron, that "the Rebbe explains: though the Torah does not limit the closeness to G-d attainable by man, we are empowered to accommodate…."[5] Particularly, we are to be appreciative of our deepest aches. Further, *Psalm* 107 notes, "let them acknowledge to Hashem His kindness and to the children of men His wonders. And let them sacrifice thanksgiving offerings, and relate his work with joyful song."[6]

We are not called upon to join with Kohanim, with kings, with Tzaddikim, or with people otherwise more lofty than ourselves. Rather, we are asked to be our best by overcoming, somehow, our lowly tendency to kvetch. We are asked to replace that tendency with the higher one of praise. The death of dear ones and other forms of intense deprivation are more than tragic to us. Consequently, such episodes are our best springboards to increased spirituality.

———————

4. Ibid.

5. Rabbi Eli Popack. "When Moses 'Consoled' Aaron." *Chabad.org.* 14 Apr. 2009 http://webcache.googleusercontent.com/search?1=cache;nUkDzmb1FScJ:www.chabad.org/blogs/blog_cdo/aid/877253/jewish/SHEMINI-When-Moses-Consoled-Aaron.htm+&c-d=10&hl=en&ct+clnk&gl=il.

6. Rabbi A. Leib Sheinbaum. "Parshas Tzav." *Peninim on the Torah.* http//www.shemayis-rael.co.il/parsha/peninim/archives/tzav77.htm.

It is incumbent upon each of us, as best as we can manage, to take up the understanding that to serve Hashem is to accept, not necessarily to like, but to acknowledge all that occurs in our lives. When we minimalize, rationalize, or deny the dreadful circumstances of our lives, we turn away from our Creator.

Rabbi Shalom Arush explains in *The Garden of Gratitude*,

> There are three types of heresy:
> The first is pure atheism, where a person doesn't believe at all in Hashem.
>
> The second type of heresy is a belief in a Higher Power, but a denial of Divine Providence. This is the denial that Hashem personally guides and governs our lives. This type of heresy is manifest by belief in happenstance and nature. It also leads to blaming others and/or self-persecution for life's setbacks and hardships.
>
> The third type is belief in Hashem and in Divine Providence, but denial that Hashem runs the world with complete loving-kindness and mercy.[7]

That is, whenever we say all that happens to us is (for our) good, we say we believe in the Boss with all of our hearts, souls, and resources. When we don't, has v'shalom, the opposite is true.

Dr Naftali Loewenthal, Lecturer in Jewish Spirituality, shares, in "Meaning and Chaos," that "redemption depicts a state of union between spiritual and physical aspects of life….Galut[, exile,] is the separation of spirit from matter."[8] We get to choose how high we extend ourselves. In view of this illumination, may we merit, on the occasion of our running to integrate our most difficult experiences, to be closer to Hashem.

---

7. Rabbi Shalom Arush. *The Garden of Gratitude*. Nanuet, NY: Feldheim, 2005.105.

8. Dr. Naftali Loewenthal. "Meaning and Chaos." *Chabad.org*. http://www.chabad.org/parshah/article_cdo/aid/43011/jewish/Meaning-and-Chaos.htm.

I didn't want to lose my pregnancy. I haven't liked the other sensations of lack with which my life has been punctuated. I am working to stay conscious, however, that all is for my good.

Amidst Oranges

Her dark eyes spoke sweet rhetoric. While I stood amidst the green grocer's oranges, a short, uniformed school girl approached me for help crossing the street.

I, too, need bridges. I struggle with a language that belongs to me and with a culture whose mores are mine. Even innocent trust, the type that aligns strangers with each other, still feels alien in my mind.

Nonetheless, in broken Hebrew, I bid the child to wait while I stopped, looked, and listened. Together, we moved from sidewalk to meridian to sidewalk. She smiled before darting to join her school friends. I'm acculturating.

Self-Actualization

Hashem defines our place by birthing us Jewish. Beyond that fact, our unrequited longings for belongingness must be worked out on a case by case, personal, basis.

More specifically, by accepting our evolving, often difficult, always wondrous, role in Creation, we Jews are capable of empowering ourselves to perceive, and to live from a starting point of great personal verity. We are able to enlighten each other about the importance of honoring each other's sacredness. We can move forward in our understandings and can actualize them not because we are, or ought to be, possessed of some particular, indefatigable human quality, but because our kind is planted in the house of G-d. Simply, we aspire to virtue because we come into this world as holy beings.

This vitality cannot be traded. It ought not to be hidden. Further, it is a shame if this blessing is compromised by our or by other folks' rubricking of it. Our job is Torah and mitzvot, not adjudication, not people pleasing, not straying, and not any manner of kowtowing to imagined strictures that have been human-sourced.

Every one of us has the potential to make our life into an altar to The Almighty and to use our thoughts, words, and deeds to glorify His Name. Every one of us will necessarily stumble in this process, yet, must proceed this way. We learn more from brushing ourselves off when we fall than from rising in a linear fashion. The critical enhancements, which can be gained from personal regression, include more acceptance, more compassion, and an increased thirst for unity. In other words, we have to reach for moral heights, while expecting, concomitantly, that the very process that raises us will subdue us and that the resulting containment, itself, will build us up.

In consequence, it is no accident that our people's route from Egypt to the Holy Land is recorded as consisting of a series of starts and stops. We might ascend and we might even merit aiding others in their aliyot, but we cannot do so without wavering. The path to personal and to tribal singularity is filled with a great variety of tribulations.

Hence, the measure of who is a Jew is not made by the determination of whether or not one's life is filled with rebbes, with pulpit rabbis, or with other forms of Talmid Chachamim. This calculation is not made by the determination of whether it is better to sponga sugary drinks off of dining room tiles in Har Nof, eat stone-oven baked challah in Afula, or to hear shiurim in Russian and in Farsi-accented Hebrew in Ashdod, rather than to clean the counters for Shabbat while glancing out a Brighton Beach window, baking challot in a modern oven in Golders Green or preparing for Pesach while shopping in a market filled with the sounds of Zulu, Xhosa, Afrikaans, and Sepedi in Johannesburg.

Our generation cannot dig the wells that our forefathers, Avraham, Yitzchak, and Yaakov dug, nor can we bring back the manna of our predecessors, who wandered the Sinai. We are not giants like Hillel or Shammai nor can we fully grasp the alien power of Bilaam, to whom Hashem, Himself, showed kindness. Each of us is merely and irreplaceably a segment of a very long, contiguous chain. That is, the computation of who each Jew is has a dynamic quality that is gauged in ethereal vessels, whose calibrations, rightfully, are beyond our understanding.

Our task, simply, is to make our lives into offerings for the quickening of Moshiach's arrival, i.e. to use our days and nights to strive toward satisfying HaKodesh Baruchu. To act otherwise, to embrace self, peer, or cultural assessments of our worth is to toss aside our most valuable attribute and to waste our most fundamental resources.

If you hear me, while stuck in traffic in Mea Shearim, turning down the volume on my Israeli folk music CDs, in deference to that community's elevation, if you see me making due without a pillow for my worn sofa or without a throw rug for my salon floor so that my resources can be spent on charity, on hospitality, or on other forms of chesed, if you witness me burgeoning with tear-felt happiness at someone else's chuppah, or crying, until nothing more can be expressed, at a levayah, or if you notice me puffing, huffing and otherwise fretting until I discover "just the right word" for a poem about the Holy Land, you will know, that in my reality, I am celebrating my Jewishness.

That Most Important Reality Show

It has become a social fancy to promote narratives, i.e. stories, through "reality"-styled accounts. Both electronic and print media, plus the more instantaneous convergent media, have availed themselves of the popularity and subsequent profitability of this trend. Everything from sanitation workers' pet shop dilemmas to rock stars' eating disorders has been made public for the sake of commerce.

What's more, this craze has anchored itself in secular, as well as in spiritual, media realms. Various soapboxes try to wow or to otherwise dazzle their readers with accounts of enemy nations' diplomats' hair styles, the amount of toilet paper certain athletes use while suffering from the flu, and aspiring "journalists" lists of retirement communities' comparative cuisines.

Whereas this nature of framing actual or enacted events is comparatively subdued in spiritual venues, this second type of broadcast, nonetheless, remains culpable for embracing the "reality" fad. Consider that religious publications have begun to feature, beyond their more typical accounts of sages' revelations and their more expected explanations of weekly Torah readings, biographies of medial breakthroughs' inventors, "anonymous" depictions of "actual" schoolyard bullying, and expert adjudications on present day dating problems. No human activity seems too trivial to share pages that also discuss *Gemara*.

In brief, whether a publication is sacred or secular, whether it focuses on how the rich and famous pay their taxes, or on how popular unions' leaders clip their fingernails, the entirety of human behavior, staged, authentic, or somewhere in-between, has become fodder for communication. Somewhere, out there, are features on dingoes dancing with neighborhood dogs, on why or why not certain sects ought to make their holiday fruit baskets look like stadiums, and on the preponderance of acne on the faces of marching band members.

Worse, not only has the public continued to revere, wittingly or not, such goings-on to the extent that juvenile hicks in North America, and elderly rulers in Europe enjoy, respectively, their own programs, but the public has fought, too, to star in reality shows. A sampling of YouTube, of Instagram, and of other social media sites demonstrate the extent to which people desire celebrity, even if such notoriety comes from washing windshields with dexterity, cleaning litter boxes with speed, or planking.

That the world attends rigorously to such "opportunities" to gain "social status" is one problem. A more grievous trouble is that while waiting in line to be collectively validated, per se, individuals ignore their own, more important, eternal "reality shows."

Hashem sees, hears, and inscribes all of our deeds. Although this world is finite, The World-to-Come is not. Moment by moment, each of us is actualizing a script that is logged and that will be used to determine our place in the cosmos. Essentially, each of us is starring in an incredibly important reality show.

If we act as though we are mindful of the filmless camera, of the never erring audio recorder, and of the never tiring verbal reportage, we might behave better. Our personal, heavenly-produced reality shows are the only spectacles that really matter.

Changing our ways so that we do acknowledge this verity is tough. Like electricity and other forms of power, Hashem's "hands," "eyes" and "ears" are not palpable. What we can't sense, we tend to ignore. It's so much easier to respond to flashy scenes offered by human media than to take action because of the consequences of future, otherworldly constructions.

Yet, the opportunity to perform for the Producer has been granted us, namely, has been placed upon us, for a limited time - the duration of each of our lives. If only we could remember that from the moment when we wake up each morning through the time when we fall sleep each night, we are being documented, we might have a chance to shine when our "realty shows" are replayed in the World to Come.

For instance, we could make an effort to begin our days with a formal (or informal) expression of gratitude for our existence. We could engage in Torah-prescribed morning rituals. We could greet our family members pleasantly. We could be careful with our spiritual and corporeal hygiene.

Sadly, if a human camera person was following us, we would probably be meticulous about all of those facets of our first waking hours. Knowing His celestial monitor is tracking us doesn't seem to make us thoughtful.

Furthermore, as we go through our days, we ought not to, deliberately or otherwise, feel relieved when a camera fails to "catch" us at being less than our best. We'd be well advised not to pick the largest fruit from the basket, literally, or figuratively, leaving the remnants for our colleagues. It would be good if we did not ignore the needs of the elderly, the pregnant, and the sick when commuting via public transportation and if we did not pretend we didn't notice our co-workers' sighs and tears. If a sound engineer held a microphone over our head, all day, we would act better than we do now, when The Almighty details, on a special audio channel, our comings and goings.

It's nasty when we walk past beggars, elbow, just a little, at lunch counters, or hang up, curtly, when friends or loved ones ring us. If an ace reporter was writing up observations about our life choices, we would act more civilly than we do now, when HaKadosh Baruchu is journaling them.

When we return home, it would behoove us to present ourselves in such a way that makes our needs equal to or less important than those of our family. We should not isolate ourselves from our spouses and children when we return, or claim a right to private time based on some semblance of self-pity. Equally inappropriate is our drinking away our work woes or drugging ourselves with foodstuffs. It's unlikely that we'd opt for those ends if we knew our actions were going to be publicized. Rather, we'd be better served to make different choices since our actions will be revealed and will be unchangeable in the next world.

The number and kind of the particulars of questions we ought to ask about our mundane behaviors is as long and as wide-ranging as is the planet's population. To some degree, they are of qualified consequence. To another degree, they are wrong, on principle. What matters is that everything we do is put on record. We are being watched, listened to, and noted. We are, every minute that we are alive, starring in the most important reality show that ever existed.

Over time, the popularity of mediated "reality" shows will wane just as have other media fads. Something shinier will take their place. The folk who had their fifteen minutes of fame will return to painting barns, to lecturing on physics, and to belly dancing. In the greater cosmic auditorium, however, no matter the favor received by Earthly kinds of reportage, those deeds will be weighed, sometimes with mercy, sometimes with justice. After all, the Greatest Documentary Maker's camera keeps rolling, tape player keeps recording, and computer keeps tabulating.

Aliyah Memories

Over the short span, during which my family and I, thus far, have merited to live in this Holy Land, I have observed a variety of differences between the Old World, i.e. Eretz Yisrael, and the New World, i.e. Europe, North America, Oceania, etc., per discourse, specifically, and per culture, in general. Although my aliyah-enhanced personal modifications have caused me to lose some of my sensitivity to distinctions between New World and Old World attitudes and values, I remain convinced that such distinctions exist. Sometimes, these disparities are challenging. Almost always, they are amusing in their oddity or unexpectedness.

Long decades ago, for instance, when my husband and I were marched to a tallit held above our heads by four men, we signed a contract and broke a glass. I circled him the requisite times and all of the sheva brachot were recited. Yet, we also had, in the back of our minds, questions about whether or not there would be any potato knishes from the reception left for him to eat after the photographer was done with us, and about what the band would sound like.

Today, I shudder to think about that type of celebration. The cost and lavishness of such a wedding's meals and of its related, subsequent parties are not essential elements to a marriage, let alone to a wedding. Rather, the middot of a couple is what's essential. Their commitment to serve Hashem, too, is essential. All else is secondary, tertiary, or of small value.

Blessedly, b'ayin tova, our children are growing up here, in this sacred land. Though I'm not sure we'll acquiesce to Missy Older's desire, to be married in Gan Sacher, a large Jerusalem park, or to her request that we serve the wedding guests only matzah and chocolate spread, I do hope that my family has adopted enough Torah values to prioritize honoring parents and teachers over worrying about whether or not we can afford to provide sushi.

Analogously, in my former life, for a long time, I was content, as a writer, with a pad and pen. An assertive newspaper editor, for whom I interned just before beginning university, snatched away those old-fashioned writing implements of mine and insisted that I compose on a typewriter. As years passed, my manual keyboard gave way to an electric one and the newspaper's production room's light boards, blue pencils, and literal cut and paste procedures yielded to more automated means of moving around paragraphs.

Some years later, my beloved husband took away my typewriter and insisted, despite my machine's ability to white out letters without correction fluid, that my tools were antiquated (only a computer cowboy would dare to mess with a diction-impassioned wife.) Anyway, that command-intense formatting software, which the love of my life insisted that I use instead of my reliable typewriter, too, was soon replaced by more sophisticated whizzywig [sic] (ought to be spelled "WYSIWYG; what you see is what you get") programs. I learned a second generation of word processing skills and determined that I was done with writing-related technology. I hadn't counted on moving to Israel.

Ironically, it is here, in this Old World, that most gadgets are chip-based. I believe we Israelis have the highest use, per capita, of cell phones. I believe that we are a leading source for software and hardware. I believe that we spend a disproportionate amount of our earnings on convergent media.

It is not so much that cell phones in The New World lack cameras, or lack the means to download IPods tones and tunes. Rather, it is the case that folk, here, will do without a sofa or a doormat in order to buy the latest gadgets or cheap similitudes thereof.

I'm not sure that I can accustom myself to local notions of relative worth. Such acculturation is a problem I can put on hold as I remain preoccupied with other discrepancies. Namely, I am busy keeping up with local strictures on raising children, I mean teenagers. Granted, in both The New World and The Old World, adolescents attend school, have activities or interests which they might or might not elect to pursue, make friends, and spend time with those friends.

However, in this Old World, unlike in other places, young adults: regularly use public transportation, frequent urban areas after dark, and are expect to be married, to be enrolled in university, and to be parenting their own small children, concurrently. I assume that the Israeli way of living evolved because our many enemies are tenacious, but our friends are true.

In New York or London, for example, if, has v'shalom, a gunman would attack, bystanders would quickly transform into fleeing civilians. Here, contrariwise, bystanders often transform into heroes. Also, here, unlike there, postsecondary schooling is for work preparation, not for parties, and so on.

Another amazing contrast between the two cultures is the social expectation governing providing for guests. Over there, it was a big deal to provide a sofa bed, or, if hosts are being generous, an entire bedroom. Here such sharing is taken for granted with the overriding conviction being that if a family is away for Shabbat or for Hag, their *entire* apartment is up for dibs, to their neighbors, who, in turn, might loan the apartment to strangers. Perhaps this mentality derives from the fact that beyond actually contemplating feeding their celebrants chocolate spread and matzah, instead of elaborate smorgasbords, locals see sma'achot as community-supported affairs.

Consider, too, the contrast in attitudes, between here and there, towards members of the military and towards law enforcement officials. There, especially in the 1960s and 1970s, anyone who participated in either of those groups earned an automatic, not-so-pretty, social onus. Here, especially in the 1960s and 1970s, anyone who participated in either of those two groups earned an automatic elevation in social status. Think "Vietnam Vets" versus "unification heroes."

Here, almost everyone's fathers, brothers, sons, and, at times, female family members, served. Here, working in law enforcement jobs or taking employment in other security fields is a natural extension of years of mandatory military training. There, such work has, historically, been seen as redneck at best, desperate, at worst.

Other areas of social separation between the two domains include strikes and boycotts. In The New World, strikes often work, but boycotts often fail; manufacturers and service providers have frequently been stymied in their attempts to replace skilled workers, while continuing to be indifferent to the needs and wants of consumers. Here, though, strikes are so frequent as to be nearly meaningless. Small concessions, if any, are the pittance yielded by an overabundance of work stoppages. Boycotts, here, though, are powerful. In this up and coming society, providers of goods and services have often been subjugated by the will of the people whose shekels they desire.

Politics, too, separate the New and Old Worlds. Over there, at least in the USA, politics are mostly focused on the intentions of two relatively similar parties. Here, an entire spectrum of human thought, from communism to socialism, to ageism, to spiritualism, and more, attempts to influence the workings of the government.

The range of political preferences here is extensive because Israel is a home to a vast amalgam of individuals. Consider, for example, that here, if one is ill,G-d Forbid, he would seek his Russian-trained physician for a diagnosis, listens to his Yemenite neighbor about the herbal cures and teshuva he needs to get healthier, all the while allowing himself to be directed by the Hungarian elder living down the street, who remains convinced that a little schnapps is all that is required for improvement. In contrast, over there, a patient would sit in line, in the waiting room of whichever doctor his HMO prescribes. That doctor would have received a roughly similar education to all of the other HMO doctors. The information available to the patient about healing his ill would be limited.

Some of the above claims are generalizations. Some of them might be based more in fancy than in fact. All of them smile at the gap between life in The New World and life in The Old World, and, hopefully, encourage people to come to this ancient one.

The Sanctity of Israel

Hashem's Cool Creations

My in-laws' Vermont vacation home has ladybugs dripping out of its faucets. In the spring, those small, valuable beetles crawl into the pipes, likely from external arteries that link the plumbing to their ground nests. Let loose, those tiny champions, all red and black wings aflutter, are hungry to chomp on household pests regardless of whether those helpful bugs enter from spigots or, more typically, from windows.

Years ago, Missy Younger developed chomping habits, too. New World spring meant, to her, time to bite into "cat whiskers," into the long strands of wild onion grass that grew in our yard. She also enjoyed tasting violets, and later, when the air shimmered with heat, day lily buds.

Sometime after Missy Younger acquired this habit, I accompanied Computer Cowboy on a business trip. Whereas, ordinarily, we avoided each other's professional activities, since my husband was completing a project for a Swiss branch of his employer, that had been years in the making, I wanted to tag along. Together, we rode on a train that took us through Alpine mountain passages and on a boat that took us across unspoiled Alpine lakes.

During other spans, when I stayed home and my husband traveled, I'd drive our little ones, all of whom were in their single digits, to the Atlantic Ocean. At that shore, my girls covered themselves up almost as much as did the Arab women, who usually sat further up the beach, and my boys slatheredthemselves and each other with sunscreen. We removed our shoes and socks and then dipped our toes and ankles into that endless expanse of waves.

Bitty bugs, tasty plants, majestic mountains, and extensive waterways all are evidence of the grandeur of Creation. It is not only the iconic sunrises over Jerusalem, or the sweet rains, which refresh the Kinneret, that are amazing. The New World's chocolate mint plants and The Old World's African, pygmy hedgehogs, likewise, are impressive. What's more, there's marvel to behold in the citrus groves of Jaffa, in the fish farms south of Haifa, and in the bee colonies of the Galilee.

It is no minor miracle when the Negev's cacti flower, when the capers, which cling to the Kotel, bloom, or when European and Indian birds, which migrate over our Holy Land, on route to Africa, and back again, fill our airways. In addition, the mountain lions and the gazelles of the Judean desert, the vipers of the Golan, and the many and varied crustaceans found near Eilat, count among the preeminences that we are blessed to witness.

Recently, my neighbor's daughter gave birth to a baby, a friend's brother recovered from radical surgery, and an acquaintance had a significant amount of vision restored via laser treatment. During that same season, a coworker's grandson took his first steps, a family in our Beit Knesset witnessed their baby become Bar Mitzvah, and a son of a dear one became engaged (not all of Creation's marvels are sensory.)

In this world of conflict and of chaos, of difficulty and of danger, there is more that is good than the opposite. We have abundant opportunities to notice The Boss' handiwork and to be grateful for the same. Hashem's cool constructions thread our lives and help us integrate ourselves in the splendor of His Way. - Hannah

****

"Look at the sky. It's sooo blue. Loook. Bluuue"

I sounded like that a couple of days ago, on a bus. I was on my way home from a sleepover that had been filled with too little sleep and too much sugar. I was pointing out the beautiful sky to my similarly oversugared and underslept friend. She smiled at me in a way that means "Rivka, you are a nut."

I get that smile a lot. I don't mind that reaction, though, as I am free to appreciate Hashem's cool creations in any way that I please, even if my choices mean that I make dumb-sounding statements on intercity buses. I'm the kind of person who brings her camera with her to school, not to take pictures of classmates, but to take pictures of flowers that are growing by the school's bus stop. I'm also the one who walks into trees because I am otherwise occupied looking at rabbits. Trees, unfortunately, are not as soft as rabbits.

Late summer nights can find me stargazing on my family's patio, trying to remember the names of constellations. I try to appreciate the most precious things in life; I try to appreciate Hashem's work.

Think about what life would be like if we had to buy oxygen at the corner store. Imagine that we wouldn't be able to breathe unless we purchased that necessary gas. If we forgot to make our run to the minimarket, we wouldn't be able to inhale. It's the simple things that we don't appreciate.

As Chana said in *Shmuel I*, "ayn tzor k'elokainu; there is no artist like our G-d." Regard the idea of a baby growing in its mother's womb or of a mother feeding it, after birth, from her body.

Things like oceans and beaches are from Hashem. Snow and rain come from the Source. The dumpster cats, which fight, at 3 a.m., every night, outside of my bedroom window, and the cockroaches, which took up residence in my friends' room during a recent class Shabbatot, as well as my friends' resulting, high pitched screams, also are from Hashem.

Basically, it's all from Him, and it's all pretty cool. *Mesilat Yesharim* and *Chovot HaLevavot* talk about this idea. The simple things are the ones we must study.

So, next time you are rushing around in life, stop to smell the bus stop flowers. - Rivka

Israel as the Foyer to a More Excellent Chamber

Our society uses perceptions of widely comprehended icons to make sense out of collective events, so comparing Israel to other iconic places, such as The Wild West, Moon Base Alpha, a spiritual retreat, and Gan Eden, can help us increase our understanding of the Holy Land. Erudition happens quickly when we start with a well-known topic and then move from it to a less familiar one.

For instance, we can conceptualize Israel as "The Wild West," as a place, where, B'ezrat Hashem, our generations can participate in the shaping of our nation's fate. "Random acts of kindness," here, influence future leaders and heroes. Deeds of faith, here, show the way, intrepidly, to everyone from lost tourists to ensconced grandmothers. In Israel, like in The Wild West, geographic boundaries have been pushed forward and not one amah of soil is given to usurpers without a fight. Like the settlements west of the Mississippi River, the settlements of the Holy Land are energized both by incredible mineral content and incredible faith. Both frontiers have seemingly unlimited natural resources, too.

Furthermore, like the denizens of the Wild West, Israel's denizens create security, not merely with guns and helicopters, but moreso with prayers and other acts of observance. Israel's pioneers, like those of the Wild West, are tested by all manner of encounters while they are, concurrently, aided by extraordinary financial, religious, and householding freedoms. The "pastoral" life of Israel is not necessarily a life of forfeiting agricultural or industrial benefits, but is one of being be led by the Ultimate Shepherd. Thus, like the Wild West, Israel is a destiny in time and place in which occupants are at once separate from and more spiritually burdened than occupants of other times and places.

Israel is also Moon Base Alpha. Many people dream of Israel. Some people visit her. Yet, few people live here. Like a moon base, Israel has a moral code that is simultaneously ascribed and implicit; only Israel's citizens truly understand how to apply her rules to their harsh and wonderful lives.

Try as government and other agencies might, both within and beyond this culture, to set down social norms for Israel, only her dwellers, those folk familiar with her plains and basins, can regularly enforce her hidden, albeit explicit laws. In this unfathomable hub, not only is justice authentically the province of the people, as realized by our service to The Boss, but it is also the case that great feats of exploration are part of this service.

Further, from the multilingual references in the Holy Land's lingo, as uniquely soldiered here, to the verbal byways of the most ancient of our kin, no one else literally, or figuratively, "understands" Israelis better than do other Israelis. In the Holy Land, it is only Israelis who perceive just what degree of caution needs to be attached to each exploit, and just who should risk their lives to make sure that tourists and residents, alike, are appropriately shielded from calculable harm.

Despite the seemingly never ending difficulties found here, Israelis are grateful for the opportunity to dwell on this soil and are proud to raise new generations of "space station" residents on this precious turf. This center of strategic operations, this Moon Base Alpha, is best peopled by the families that build and nurture it.

Beyond being the Wild West, or a moon base, Israel is a spiritual retreat. At this holy site, tacit behavior incompliant with existent purposes or with the institutional processes of other cultures, which simultaneously (and temporarily) refutes the value of the undergirding principles of modern society, is de rigueur. Israelis do not answer to rules derived from idolatrous religions, nor do we seek to become a nation that conforms to the wiles of the dollar, the euro or the yen.

In Israel, not only do residents throw off the entrapments of other nations, but we also cast away the glamours of our acculturated selves. Here, people are not writing teachers and critics of writing, for instance, but are writers; we are not architects, but carpenters. We are not oblivious participants, but active contributors.

Many immigrants to this great land drop their New World names in order to reclaim their Old World ones. Most immigrants similarly yield their New World sensibilities to Old World ones. Israel, the greatest of spiritual retreats, is a place where folk reclaim individual and national distinctiveness. Israel remains a place for self-betterment in that it affords much support for spiritual searching, finding, and evolving.

Because Israel is authentic, Israel is not just the Wild West, Moon Base Alpha, or a spiritual retreat. The Holy Land is also Gan Eden.

Israel is blissful; nothing feels as good as does calling into existence one's purpose for living. This Holy Land is the manifestation of the highest forms of beauty and eminence. In this rare place, populated by individuals regularly reaching, discovering, and metamorphosing, humanity's glory is at its most intense.

Because all kinds of brilliance is continuously being developed here, Israel is humankind's foyer to an even more excellent "chamber." It is to her that Moshiach will introduce wonders. It is here that the Third Temple's brilliance and magnificence will be experienced. It is here that Heaven holds close to Earth.

Israel is the Wild West. Israel is Moon Base Alpha. Israel is a spiritual retreat. Israel is Gan Eden. Israel is forever.

Israel as the Wild West

"The Wild West" refers to the geographic edge of North America's "civilized" communities during the late 1800's. Whereas the Wild West is often thought of, in the language of popular culture, as having been inimitably concerned with that time/place's management of grazing domestic livestock, "cowboy" paths to livelihood were and continue to be important money-making routes in many parts of the world.

Many herders of large animals worked, and still work, elsewhere on the globe. These groups include: the cattle gauchos of the South American pampas; the goat herders of North Africa; the drovers, i.e. sheep men, of Australia; the camel herders of Mongolia, as well as the boarder-free, horse breeding, Bedouins. Wherever large, sparsely populated, tracts of land are accessible, humans have translated those parcels into economic gains.

Further, the main North American cattle grazing area was known as "The West" mostly because European settlers moved from the eastern seaboard, westward, until stymied by the Pacific Ocean. In contrast, indigenous North Americans roved relatively more locally, and Asians migrated to the States, from island nations in the Pacific, eastward.

Moreover, that area was known as "wild," because life beyond established communities tended to be rowdy, unruly, and otherwise rough. Such a life possessed scant allusions to more typical: human development, social complexity, or urban sprawl. Social deviance, in such circumstance, was monitored by "local" enforcement agencies, rather than by traditional authorities, and was often comprised of: violent crime, unequal representation in the adjudication process, and the exploitation of natural and human resources, especially as enacted by bandits that opportunistically killed naïve, or poorly armed citizens. In such collectives, people: killed off their predecessors and repossessed their worldly wealth; experienced frequent damage and danger from animal predators; lived through exacerbations of their own and of their peers' neurotic and psychotic tendencies, as those tendencies were provoked by participants' seminomadic lifestyle; and were subjected to the frustration of reaching the geographic limit of their frontier.

On the other hand, "The Wild West" has been imprinted in popular culture memory because that region's occupants had the chance to: shape the destiny of a nation; push forward geographic boundaries; benefit from seemingly unlimited natural resources; aid national security; enjoy extraordinary financial, religious, and householding freedoms, live a pastoral (rather than an agricultural or industrial) life, and fulfill their understanding of Manifest Destiny. Citizens of "The Wild West" were at once separate from and "superior" to greater society's members.

Like the Wild West, Israel, a Middle Eastern country, relative to the currently dominating cultural yardsticks of Europe and of North America, can seem rowdy, unruly, and otherwise rough. The Old World's approach to literacy, to the quality of life, and to life expectancy, for instance, differs vastly from the approach of the Newer World. While this society's fabric provides fewer incidents of misdemeanor crimes, ayin tova, in a good eye (given this society's tendency toward close-knit communities), than does the fabric of newer societies, this society's seemingly blurred definition of "social deviance," combined with this society's seemingly greater number of nonnormative members, makes Israel's felons and Israel's response to them, seem baser. After all, the court system here is still evolving - it's still developing poise and equity.

Some Israelis, furthermore, selfishly and unethically, take advantage of our resources, from man to *Melocactus sp.,* "melon cactus." What's more, a vigilante mentality, toward religious and civil law enforcement, flourishes in this land. As well, a minority continues to victimize this society's easily deluded or physically weak members. Plentiful data indicates, too, that the local government has a role in disrupting settlements, and that native creatures sometimes threaten farm animals. As for Israeli society's contributions to the population's mental disorders, studies have shown that limitless sunshine, single-handedly, can make people crazy.

On the flip side, Israel, more than any other society, has good reason for being legendary. People living in this quintessential bridge between Africa and Asia have a more remarkable ability to shape the destiny of their nation than do people in most other places. Further, whereas most settlers were limited by mountains or rivers, Israel's settlers enjoy a spiritually infinite frontier Also, Israel remains a font of life. She features many ecosystems and multitudes of biological miracles. Concomitant with her diversity, Israel has many economic openings, too. Plus, Israelis play an active role in their national security; most residents have served in the nation's armed forces and reserves, and many remain active, licensed owners of firearms.

Other benefits of Israeli society, akin to the benefits of living in "The Wild West," include, but are not limited to: greater than usual laxity per finances, religious freedom, householding freedom, abundant prospects for living a pastoral life, and the chance to fulfill Manifest Destiny. Israelis are distinct from members of other societies as Israeli social status is not one of strata climbing, but of international service.

It is not so much that sprawling ranches are synonymous with sand dune realities or that salon girls have much in common with tznius women. Rather, it is the case that Israelis, akin to the real and exaggerated inhabitants of "The Wild West," comprise a society that is "larger than life' both because of its ruggedness and its opportunities for self-actualization.

Israel as Moon Base Alpha

In developing nations, the understanding of the meaning of "frontier" was eventually extended from that of "areas within contiguous landmasses, which are situated at the edge of ordinary civilization," to "areas not necessarily on landmasses, which are situated at the edge of ordinary civilization." The ocean is one such frontier. Space is another.

Israel, hence, is not only comparable to "The Wild West," but is also comparable to places where space exploration has taken place. Making aliyah is considered as much of a cutting edge endeavor as is venturing beyond Earth. Like space stations, contemporary Israeli is: a hub for local exploration, a juncture for further adventures, a residence, and a center of strategic operations. "Israel as Moon Base Alpha," is a suitable rhetorical vehicle for conveying the experience of living in The Holy Land.

Israel is a hub for exploration, both as "exploration" is understood as involving "a methodical search within an existent social system," and as "exploration" is understood as involving a "methodical search beyond an existent social system." Just as members of lunar colonies will one day examine the moon, itself, and the stars, to which the moon refers, Israelis examine both their known world, Creation, and the world to which Creation refers.

In Israel, physical discovery is important. Israel remains on the forefront of innovations in medicine, in agriculture, in technology, in geology, and more. Drip irrigation advancements, computer imaging technology, as well as breakthroughs in treating both burn victims and trauma victims, are among the many globally lauded social advances originating here. As a result, like a lunar civilization that enjoys prosperity indigenous to its being able to export priceless moon materials to other communities, Israel enjoys prosperity indigenous to her being able to export priceless research to humanity.

Several reasons are popularly touted for Israel's atypical success in science. These explications could be equally plausibly for the atypical successes in lunar colonies and include: people are necessarily inventive under circumstances of limited resources; people are necessarily more cross-fertile when operating within a small physical domain, i.e. within a geographically tiny area; and certain workplace environs, i.e. the degree of holiness of this land, create unusually favorable work conditions.

This land's holiness not only impacts her joining together of great science, but moreso impacts her joining together of monumental spirituality. The advantages of engaging in inward-focused questing, in Israel, have been broadcast by all three of the major, monotheistic religions for millennia. There is no secret that sensory and extrasensory realizations are heightened on this precious turf, the contemporary world's sudden myopia notwithstanding. Various, vying histories of civilization recognize this nation's longstanding spiritual eminence. Just like the moon is unique in its relationship to the Earth, Israel is unique its relationship to the other nations.

Beyond being a bastion for progressive scientific and spiritual growth, Israel, parallel to a lunar colony, serves as a springboard for other journeys. Lunar bases are predicted to be utilized for hyperspace exploration as well as for housing Earthly militia. Analogously, Israel has long functioned as a launch pad for ventures related to her interests as well as has long been exploited by external militaries seeking Israel's proximity to active fields of combat, and to her light policing of hazardous goods and of extremely risky behaviors (e.g. harboring, and even funding, enemies within her borders).

Governments that eventually make use of the moon will do so for similar reasons why they currently make use of Israel. Consider that Israel entices newcomers to her "unusual and exciting society" and that she possesses broadmindedness toward questionable domestic and global relations. Israel is, among other things, a place for international intrigue.

International maneuvering aside, another way in which Israel is akin to planned space stations is her characteristic of being a place of "simple" residency. Not all undertakings on the moon, or within Israel, are those with uncertain outcomes. In space and in the Holy Land, alike, the magnitude of tolerance of social deviance must be tempered by the survival requirements of the colonists. Social structures like space colonies and like our sovereign Jewish nation must, concurrent with their roles as research havens and political treasures, unify their dissimilar indigenous factions in order to enhance their and humanity's future survival.

The moon is not merely a way station for Earthly rustlers and bandits any more than Israel is merely a stopover for politically ambitious leaders. Both Moon Base Alpha and Israel necessarily must serve as homes to "ordinary" families and to those families' subsequent generations. Societies in both places must incorporate provisos for the rest of humanity, too, in case of cataclysmic events. That is, both our future moon bases and our existent Holy Land must hold fast to certain social rules, while concurrently punting norms that could endanger their denizens.

The immediate gratification of greater society is not always a sufficient reason to sacrifice colonists. Moon dwellers ought no more to throw themselves off of their rock-encrusted satellite to save the pockets of rich, Earthly manufacturers than Israeli ought to willingly march to her own destruction to back the opinions expressed by foreign authorities.

Yet, foreign authorities continue to converge on Israel because Israel, like a space station, is strategic to their operations. Despite the fact that Israelis have historically and repeatedly publicized that their protectorate's governor is the Big Boss, world leaders bent on global supremacy continue to try to dominate our special real estate. Politicians of all nationalities and stripes contend that their presence, here, is necessary because "keeping us company" provides them with opportunities to: deter their foes' actions, maintain surveillance of those foes, protect their regional investment, and defend those investments against aggressors.

Often those decision-making and regulatory process commanders forget to include in their computations that local inhabitants have made great sacrifices to live here and that we don't plan to meekly yield to alien sovereignties. Since we locals are a heterogeneous people, an amalgamation of individuals from dissimilar societies, whose diversity, itself, helps protect us from unfavorable suasory and coercive actions, we're unlikely to embrace would-be despots. Rather, we aim to remain in control of our nation, to rely on our own strictures.

Israel, like a theoretical moon base, is: an "undomesticated" place, an incubator for exploration, a jumping off spot for great adventures, a harbor for fringe deviants and for general risky goings-on, and a domain from which world conquest can be facilitated. However, Israel is simultaneously a sanctuary for humanity, a source of wondrous expertise, and a bastion of integrity. It's not enough to use big guns to become an overlord, here.

Israel as a Spiritual Retreat

Living in Israel means departing from cultural norms established in other geographies and eras. Whereas most parts of the globe sprouted and continue to sprout societies derived from Christian, Islamic, or polytheistic standards, our tiny, Holy Land sprouts a society based on the mingled values of contemporary and ancient Judaism.

In the past, and, IYH, in the near future, customarily benevolent monarchs dictated and will dictate Israel's governance, as outlined by Torah's social blueprint. Today, as we await Moshiach, the canons of the Holy Land are tinged by other sources. Whereas Jewish holidays prescribe our calendar, Jewish dictums prescribe our actions and our manner of speaking, Torah is not yet our lone navigational instrument. Rather, Israeli truth is compromised by rules derived from human "intelligence," especially as those rules are understood through human passions.

Hence, it is not only Israelis who are mystified by the state of things in Israeli society, but outsiders, too. That is to say, individuals, who are culturally detached from the day-to-day goings-on of this country, e.g. visitors, newcomers, and remotely operating observers, are confused about the quality of our national distinctiveness.

Contemporary Israel is not favorably branded in the world's media. Given the lack of a consistent local frame for "Israeliness," outsiders have been able to impose their prejudices onto our essence, i.e. they have been able to evaluate our nation according to their social constructs rather than according to ours. This behavior, on a good day, is analogous to a bald eagle judging a Galapagos cormorant on the basis of flight or to a penguin evaluating an roadrunner on the basis of swimming prowess; ontologically dissimilar systems ought not to be used to evaluate each other, in general, and measures not based on Torah ought not to be used to evaluate Israel, more exactly.

Israelis should exert themselves to moving from being largely externally defined, to being largely internally defined. Toward that end, I offer up an idea; Torah.

The problem is that the world, for the most part, fails to grasp that Israel's reproduction of The Master Social Engineer's Word extends over and throughout life. Consequently, rhetorical pabulum is needed.

Outsiders weigh that Israel's self-account lacks zest (hence, the current tourist bureau's mistaken attempt to market this country as a place for hot sex.) Whereas an insipid account is one to which no one is going to pay attention, any secular framing of this nation still needs to be constructive.

For those reasons, I propose that the absolute essence, the phenomenology of Israel, be articulated through literary devices. While the warmongers and the other species of profiteers continue to pander via slanted media feeds and via other shiny trinkets of social modulation, the rest of us can reject their appeals to lower tastes and can reject their subsequent exploitation of underdeveloped minds. Our verbal ombudsmen can be of our choosing rather than of theirs.

Granted, "Israel as Literature" has already been manifested in countless works of fiction and even in a few movies. Nonetheless, insufficient amounts of sympathetic, creative nonfiction, that is, of suasory essays, have been generated to route public opinion.

It's timely and useful for Israel to step beyond the overabundance of existent worldly texts and minority-interest political-economical misgivings. We need a complimentary face on "Israeliness" and an improved global grasp of our land's logical, existential, and metaphysical qualities.

Literary devices, like extended metaphor: have universal function, rely on shared language as their agent, and are sufficiently powerful to enable their users to analyze, interpret, and critique the observable facts to which these devices are applied. Presenting the significance of "Israeliness" via such vehicles would involve presenting a readily and widely intelligible, cheaply replicated and easily dispersed, and perceivably appraisable understanding of our nation.

Comparisons between Israeli and other societies are a regular part of the global culture lexicon. At best, these comparisons: titillate us into questioning the propriety of assumptions about our society, stimulate mental images, cause indignation, and, perhaps, increase patriotism. At worst, they illuminate just how poorly our rhetorical assets look as mirrored in the global ideological dressing room.

Consider that a variety of rhetorical tropes can be used to illuminate "Israeliness." Such a direct comparison of one thing to another, e.g. of Israel to a spiritual retreat, derives its power from the familiarity that a broad audience has with an original subject matter. For instance, the parameters of "spiritual retreatness" are defined both by tales that appear true and by tales that are false, as opposed to only by truths. That's why comparing "Israeliness" to a spiritual retreat has the potential to make Israeliness more comprehensible.

More specifically, Israel's nature can seem less enigmatic if we think of Israel as a place where individuals can safely remove themselves from commonplace experiences for the purpose of improving their personal or our global welfare. This concept is easy to absorb since Israel is a place where reflection and prayer occur naturally; Israel is a place of great kedusha.

Sometimes, people are forced, by extenuating circumstances, ranging from loved ones' compassion to judges' edicts, to engage in internal exploration. Other times, people choose internal exploration for themselves. Even if folk only seek spiritual relief for self-assessed tensions, there remain, as expressed by R.K. Merton, in *Social Theory and Social Structure*,[9] several ways in which to deal with those pressures; "conformity," "ritualism," "innovation," "rebellion," or, as per this essay's focus, "retreatism."

"Conformity," tacit behavioral compliant to a given culture's goals and institutional means, does not always resolve socially-provoked stressors. Not everyone is willing to deal with their problems by smiling and nodding. Think about the array of regular reactions to: bombs in our literal backyards, high taxation, irregularly enforced driving laws, and messy post office lines.

9. Robert K. Merton. *Social Theory and Social Structure*. New York Free Press, 1967.

"Ritualism," tacit behavioral compliant to a given culture's institutional means, concurrent with divergence from that culture's social aims, too, is an unsatisfactory response to all socially-induced stressors. Not everyone is willing to reorganize their lives in order to avoid dissonance. Not all of us, as exemplified by the plighted Gush Katif settlers, willingly relocate/organize civil protests, rather than instigate a near civil war, when kicked out of our homes. Not all of us, as exemplified by the individuals who challenge the Jerusalem gay parade, by toasting trash cans, willingly endanger human life.

"Innovation," tacit behavioral compliant with a given culture's foci, concurrent with divergence from that culture's institutional means of achieving those foci, too, is an often unfulfilling response to socially-induced dissonance. Only a portion of the population has the resources, the willingness, *and* the opportunity to catapult themselves beyond normal organizational constraints. Everyone else is otherwise weighted and must make do with less innovative problem solving.

Consider transplanted academics reduced to teaching in: distance learning programs, private workshops, and corporate venues. Reflect, too, on olim driven to self-limiting resource allocation, e.g. to relying mostly on English-language listservs, rather than on broader resources, in their attempts to better acclimate, e.g. to stop paying "special American prices." This strategy, as well, does not always work.

"Rebellion," tacit behavior not compliant with existent cultural aspirations and existent institutional means, but grounded in a value for the society in question, similarly, has a quickly approached threshold of utility. For example, the Kadima Party poised itself as a fresh alternative to extant Israeli political parties/ideological platforms, but functioned more like the Likud Party, of which it was an offshoot. Also, a recent university students' strike, a daring attempt to get beyond previous, disappointing faculty bargaining strategies, succeeded in drawing public attention to faculty grievances, but did not gain faculty more concessions than had traditional work stoppages.

When conformity, ritualism, innovation, and rebellion, singularly, or in combination, fall short of alleviating socially-induced dissonance "retreatism," tacit behavior not compliant with existent cultural ambitions and institutional means, which renounces, at least temporarily, the value of the undergirding principles of the society in question becomes an option. New World, "retreatists" include: persons living "beyond the grid," mystics, and drug addicts. Old World "retreatists" include: nomads, spiritualists, and hashish smokers, as well as a large number of more "ordinary," i.e. merged into the dominant culture, souls.

Whereas many cases that seem, superficially, to be instances of "retreatism" are, in fact, cases of "rebellion," or of "innovation," respectively, e.g. kids who "escape" to the Middle East to break from their families of origin, and e.g. scientists who search out the intellectual community here for purposes of furthering their personal research agendas, there remain a substantial per cent of people living in or visiting Israel who dwell here for reasons of releasing themselves from old social norms and agencies. Examples of actual retreatists include some: lone soldiers, yeshiva students, and foreign volunteers (the classification of these individuals depends largely on their rationale for coming to Israel.)

In their process of reprogramming themselves, visa via the fresh understanding of the nature of social constraints and freedoms that their experiences within Israel provide, these individuals often seek to operate within closed, and custodial, systems. They also often seek extraordinary experiences.

Most people whom retreat within Israel are pleased that the chose the Holy Land as the locale for their personal evolutions. Both government and private organizations are lush with statistics on people who made aliyah because they had earlier visited Israel "to find themselves," regardless of whether their discoveries occurred in connection with a simcha, a corporate-sponsored trip, or a year of study abroad. Likewise, there exist many accounts, both anecdotal and statistically rigorous, which indicate that folk already dwelling here find that this land inspires them to climb their personal madregot, i.e. inspires them to try to find means for privately and significantly bettering themselves. For some people, the entirety of the nation is a place of spiritual retreat, so sensitive are those persons to the kedusha concomitant to every four amot. For other people, special circumstances bring about their heightened sense of self. Reschooling one's self in Israel, calculatedly or otherwise, is rewarding. The many entrepreneurs, whom have arrived at Israel's shores, only to trade their suits for tzitzis, have not been disappointed in the improvement of their physical health and spiritual growth. Youths that have flocked to Israel's cities and outposts, in pursuit of indifferent sex, casual drugs, and ubiquitous rock and roll, have often healed themselves by filling their empty spaces with chesed, with kosher food, and with harmonies intoned by their emerging souls. Visitors, who thought they came for relics, frequently leave sated by antiquities of a greater kind. Tourists looking for exotic experiences often find themselves redirected toward the mysteries and fascinations of their private worlds.

In making themselves vulnerable to actualizing personal change, here, many, many people have received, in this land of spiritual retreat, answers to their questions about how to maintain a society, as well as answers to their questions about how to maintain themselves. It is valuable to see the Holy Land as not only a haven from ordinary social exigencies and personal problems, but also as a locale where personal metamorphosis can and frequently does take place. "Israeliness" as "Spiritual Retreat" is a useful metaphor.

Israel as Gan Eden

There exist divergent commentaries as to the exact location of Garden of Eden. Some say The Garden of Eden is located on Earth, some say in Heaven, and some say on Earth and in Heaven, simultaneously. Yet, there is agreement that Gan Eden is valuable to acquire. Israel, too, is valuable to acquire.

Both Gan Eden and Israel are places for: self-betterment, partaking in ultimate bliss, and experiencing idealized beauty and glory. In addition, both Gan Eden and Israel exist as foyers to even more excellent chambers.

Per self-betterment, the type that results from individual effort, as well as the type that is a result of environment, Israel has traditionally been iconicized as a locale for psychic and physical healing. From the holy influence of Tsfat to the curative waters and sands of the Dead Sea, Israel is celebrated for its healing powers.

Further, like Gan Eden, Israel is legendary for providing its inhabitants with amazing varieties of contentment. Given that rapture derives, in part, from the ability to get beyond the confines of ordinary cognitive processes, it is of little wonder that bliss is regularly experienced in Israel, a place of limitless explorations of the nonintellectual frontier. Since sensory and extrasensory responsiveness is heightened in this precious domain, which is much more of a facilitator of immense, otherworldly discoveries than are other places, Israel is much more of a facilitator of intense joy than are other settings.

Here, we can focus on the ecstasy associated with: a rich dessert, a splendid symphony, a softly-colored sunset, a wisp of summer wind (especially if that wind is blowing during a heat wave), and the scent of lavender. All contemplation in Israel is enhanced by the innate quality of her holiness.

Likewise, Israel is akin to Gan Eden in terms of Israel being a location of idealized exquisiteness and glory. Nine tenths of all of the world's beauty is conferred upon this realm. Similarly, honor and distinction have been disproportionately granted to this area for the entirety of Israel's existence. World history and literary texts document a plethora of cultures that have sought to conquer Israel, not only because of the land's strategic worth, but also because of the land's grandeur. Israel's allure has long been the ultimate fascination because Israel is the ultimate excellence. Dwelling here is the golden dream.

Israel is famous, as well, for its service as an antechamber to the most important section of The Boss's palace. As this planet's spiritual vortex, Israel is esteemed for its ability to transition Earthly people and things from the mundane to the sacred. As Earth's energetic epicenter, Israel is the bridge to a higher dominion. When people make aliyah, they "go up," i.e. they approach the greatest spiritual point on Earth.

Whereas it is not possible, in the course of this lifetime, to experience Gan Eden, it is possible to experience Israel. When we call to mind that this remarkable land is at once a place of: self-betterment, bliss, magnificence, and access to the highest domain, we are able to understand Israel as paradise.

More about Island Living

I remain uncertain as to whether Israel is, per select sociopolitical lens, a continental island, that is, an entity that rests on a continental shelf (discounting our current rulers' predilection for relying, on a particular large, foreign sovereignty for directions on decision-making), or whether she is, per other select sociopolitical associations, a volcanic island, a three thousand year-old plus source of seamounts and of habitations fixed in a constellation-like pattern. It's useful to explore both possibilities.

If it is the case that Israel can most accurately be compared to a continental island, it helps to take into account that in the physical world, Israel sits on the Arabian Plate, which is moving toward the Eurasian Plate. Geologists teach that our literal land mass, which is currently dominated by our ethnic cousins, and our figurative land mass, which is likewise currently dominated by those cousins' ideologies and by their less tacit, but more immediate, potent, forms of conquest, is on a collision course with a significant chunk of the civilized world.

The science of the lithosphere aside, it has already been noted that our cousins' material (think "oil") and cultural influence (think "recurring features on their lifestyle, published in places like *The New York Times*") have spread into, or have otherwise transformed, the boundaries of many nations and the matchlessness of many internationally powerful people. Like tectonic plates crashing against other formative features of the outermost stratum of inner Earth, our kin's actions cause "earthquakes," "volcanic activity," and the formation of both "mountains" and "oceanic trenches."

More interesting is that earth science explains such occurrences, when they are found in nature, as deriving from temperature differentials between the Earth's cool, rigid surface structure and the Earth's hotter, mechanically weaker, underpinnings. Essentially, physical shifts among the earth's most accessible layers take place when our planet needs to "blow some steam," i.e. when our planet needs to disperse some built up energy. Hence, it seems uncanny that world citizens are surprised each time our cousins violate a "strain threshold."

To add a little charif to these thoughts, consider Dr. Uri ten Brink's claim, espoused in "Peace and Science in the Middle East," that "the Dead Sea Valley is not a true tectonic rift, but is [a strike-slip fault system,] a continental transform that laterally offsets the Arabian tectonic plate against [another] tectonic plate."[10] It's as if The Boss bookmarked our homeland as a spot for future action. In other words, watch this space, *and* don't stop praying.

Practically speaking, it's not so much that The New World ought to be concerned about California falling into the ocean" as it is that The New World ought to be concerned about the advance of distant tectonics. Interestingly, the scientifically predicted time for this forthcoming, grand geophysical conflagration matches the spiritually predicted time for the forthcoming, grand sociopolitical conflagration that heralds Moshiach.

Consider, too, that if Israel can be seen as an island, she might be the volcanic type. It doesn't require a lot of imagination to picture the Holy Land as a system of submerged volcanoes, flat-topped or otherwise, which once stood above "the surface," or to picture the Holy Land as an assemblage of habitations.

There are many aberrations on our Earth's mantle, including calderas, which have their genesis in much earlier goings-on. Over millennia, peaks have risen and sunk due to many forces.

Analogously, Israel's social landscape is full of pockmarks. Such "geographic" features hold clues as to why, during the period of our celebrating the anniversaries of Jerusalem's unification and of our state's existence, concurrent with our cousins' announcement, to the world, that they have, has v'shalom, plotted our demise, our leaders, in turn, propose to amputate all but Israel's most necessary geographies.

---

10. Dr. Uri ten Brink. "Peace and Science in the Middle East." *IRIS/SSA Distinguished Lectureship.* 2008. https://woodshole.er.usgs.gov/project-pages/dead_sea/.

Whether by gun or by bulldozer, in the past, we defended ourselves. At present, we seem to be pushing each other over for the right to claim the title of "Greatest Profferer of Ignoble Fear in the Face of Danger to the Nation." That our former glory has gone under water is plainly perceptible. Moreso, the world's response, to our self-induced political plummeting, is to cast our nation into the role of "newly accessible" (namely, free-for-the-raping) reef. We would do better without such "natural features" or unnatural "understandings."

Beyond topography, volcanic islands are defined as being constituted by noncontiguous communities. To grasp how this aspect of the Israel-as-volcanic-island analogy holds, one merely has to weigh the plethora of international charts created to project the pieces into which our nation would be divided by "interested parties" (if we continue to allow ourselves to be diagrammed by outsiders, we will be cut into more pieces than postwar Berlin.)

It is bad enough that we force our residents to abide by a system of mapping which makes us drive on walled highways of various externally-named sovereigns' designations. We ought to be able to access ALL of our land, and we ought to do away with agents that would kill us. Proponents of the Israel-as-volcanic-island model argue that Israel's free sale yielding of geographic and of other types of (ad)vantages is in Israel's interest; becoming increasingly similar to an archipelago means we can more readily emulate the celebrated world dominance of other island chains such as Great Britain or Japan.

Those "supporters" are mistaken; we Israelis are neither interested in conquest nor in being relegated to a chapter of history. Whereas it is fact that empires, like Great Britain and like Japan, ruled land masses disproportionately larger than them, it is also the case that archipelagos are formed when mountain apexes are submerged due to the results of tectonic plates sliding over erupting, subterranean hot spots. Such redefinition of world politics is hardly in our interest.

Whether a continental island, or a volcanic one, Israel is truly surrounded by a sea of adversaries. It's fortunate that we continue to look to Hashem to guide us.

The Music

Yes, I love this country. I love: listening to Shlock Rock lyrics about "Modeh Ani," reading about Rashi in daily newspapers, and hearing the literal siren that calls us to observe Shabbat. There are also other reverberations, here, that stir me. I am also roused by Israel's acoustic/psychic echo of sma'achot, of holidays, and of children.

The resonating excellence of sma'achot is not the actual notes and rests woven by their music. Rather, celebrations' true vibration is their quivering of our neshemot. For example, at a recent seudah Bar Mitzvah, most of us gasped in delight when witnessing several dozen boys literally run to make merry on the dance floor. Beyond typical hugs and pats, those youths used their bodies to convey joy, enthusiasm, and otherworldly radiance. Whereas their faces glistened in equal parts sweat and ecstasy, those boys' inner selves shone from timeless consecration.

Similarly, at a recent chatana, we attendees were privileged to a rapture-driven glimpse of paradise. Young, and not-so-young men attending that important event put their entireties into celebrating their friend, the chatan, and his new wife, the kallah. Those light-filled faces belonged to IDF soldiers, to hesder yeshivot students, and to middle-aged (!) fellows, but their souls resided elsewhere, in immutable spheres not ordinarily visited.

In a mechitzah-separated space, those men's womenfolk, likewise, glimmered. Their feminine élan flowed from the kallah's tisch, to the bedecken, to the chuppah, and on into the night. With sighs and shouts (it's challenging to describe the Sephardi call for blessing; that primitive-sounding, often slurred, set of munificent words usually resonates like a primordial trill), the women of the wedding, not the least of whom were members of the actual wedding party, summoned goodness to fasten itself to the newly married.

Analogously, at another evening, at sheva brachot for a different young pair, luminosity was again the primary trait manifested by the participants. Chareidim in gorgeous, long payot, businessmen with shorter, careful locks, and serious-appearing yeshuvniks, animatedly bowed and swayed in welcoming a new Jewish home into the midst of our nation. The men's vim was palpable. Their conjugated voices raised the rest of us attendees to unnatural places.

It is difficult to step away from such bliss-filled moments. After the Bar Mitzvah, for instance, one of my own children labeled me "spoilsport" for wanting to leave "too soon." All ages can sense the heighted nature of such special events, and all ages, appropriately so, are hesitant to exit them.

After the wedding, many of the lofty celebrants lingered, singing aloud even when the band had gone home. Their acapella bursts wrapped around us guests returning to the parking lot. After the sheva brachot, too, lay musicians beat additional syncopations on their darabukas and strummed additional chords on their guitars - they seemed indifferent to the fact that their hosts were wiping down tables and folding up chairs.

Propitiously, this sma'achot-sourced euphoria exists beyond those circles. I'm thinking, specifically, of the birthday part of a friend's son.

I cried when I saw the pictures of that event. Those colorful frames show the total immersion, in the moment, of many young boys.

Similarly, I cried when regarding the butterfly energy of the many limbs of the small girls that attended Missy Younger's Bat Mitzvah celebration. That dynamism that lingered in the hall, even after the last of those little lovelies has been bundled up and taken home was sparkly; it was eternal.

Often, high spirits are built from "simple" song and laughter. Fortunately, such "sma'achot music" abounds in our lives. We are blessed, for example, that such heavenly kisses are also showered upon us during Mo'ed.

During religious festivals, it is not merely that our load is lighter, as ordained by religious law, but it is simultaneously true that our enjoyment is heightened, as equally provided for by religious law. As hosts and as visitors, during Mo'ed, our capacity to appreciate the "tones" that surge toward us from the ultimate sphere is increased.

I remember one Mo'ed when two of our guests spooned up every drop of an otherwise accidentally melted desert. Whereas the taste was probably good (Missy Older had made the sweet treat), their savoring of it was more about the situation than about the sugar; after dessert we needed to pray thanks, and then, after Birkat Hamazon, to disband to once more take care of mundane things. Thus, the guests' relishing of those last spoonfuls of our shared meal was their means of drawing out the music heard via our Mo'ed access to the celestial symphony.

By the same token, another Mo'ed, when I was the guest rather than the host, an afternoon's breeze, temperate sunlight, and my host's abundance of sukkah cushions harmonized with "the music." That my friend's husband was learning Torah at an adjacent table, and that the smell of verbena wafted toward us, too, enhanced the moment. My time in that sanctuary-built-from-light was remarkably tuneful.

Of course, otherworldly melodies gain access to our domain during full holidays. That those tunes, rooted in places beyond our ken, are indigenous to extraordinary times is known. Think of the music of Hanukkah, recall the joyful tunes of Tu B'Av, and savor your memories of the harmonies of Rosh Chodesh.

Less frequently, but still often enough, we connect with enchantments concomitant to our regular days. It would have been difficult for me, for instance, not to have sung to the music of my children's development.

When Missy Older, for example, brought a variety of new schemes to my attention, the corners of my mouth turned up. Whether her plotting involved a fresh system for allocating chores, a fresh strategy for raising money to visit The Old World, or a new plan for convincing me to allow her to stay up late to chat with her friends, I necessarily had to create an accompaniment to the resulting heavenly music. Children's tilting at convention is surprisingly euphonious.

What's more, although seemingly "ordinary," the music that leaked out of Older Dude, when he was preoccupied with sacred wonder, was equally profound. I recall him bounding into my family's salon to share insights from the *Gemara* on proper sukkah dimensions. It was delightful to hear his lecture on a queenly convert's sukkah needs, especially in the context of him failing to notice his neglect of measures – the kid had outgrown his shirt, but hadn't noticed. Of this obliviousness, too, I sang gratitude; one verse celebrated my son's Torah knowledge and another celebrated his health.

Missy Younger, in her innocence of worldly surfeit, too, inspires song. One Hanukkah, I was treated to viewing Tel Aviv through her mostly unsullied eyes. By paying attention to my younger daughter's musical mode, I was able to enjoy an otherwise less-than-wholesome city's offerings. My focus was redirected to lush trees, to pretty parks, and to clean sidewalks. I was able to appreciate Tel Aviv's many fountains, marvelous pedestrian overpasses, and abundant shopping centers (Missy Younger proclaimed that shopping is as "pure" as is sunlight and that Dizengoff Center Mall, being easily twice the size of Jerusalem's Malha Mall, is a natural wonder.) In the company of such a blameless soul, I was compelled to accompany the hallowed chorus.

Younger Dude's music tends to be improvisational. His energy elevates us. When I look at that little guy's face and at the faces of our short neighbors, with whom Little Dude practically lives, all is good in the world. He glories when those small children and their slightly older siblings play with him. When they reach out their sticky-fingered warmth to engage him in high-pitched Hebrew, he reflects majesty. When those little friends "rescue him" from our "boring," teenager-dominated home, he is ecstatic. Only the most "hearing-impaired" would fail to perceive his happy music.

There is a kind of good in the universe, that, if we listen carefully, we can hear. When attending Sma'achot, when celebrating Mo'ed and holidays, and when taking joy in our children, we are assisted in that effort. All we need to do is to sing along.

Rain

Baruch Hashem, as I type these words, it is pouring outside. The Israeli countryside, from North to South, is soaking up The Almighty's gift of rain.

In the beginning, there was no rain. Only during the second segment of that singular week, that period which was composed of seven inscrutable days, did Hashem separate the heavenly waters from the waters below. Before that, He fashioned space, time and light. That is, the vessels for the waters of the upper chamber were made before those exalted waters, themselves, came into being.

Neither flora nor fauna were created before rain existed. Specifically, dry land and plants were brought into existence on Day Three, sea creatures and birds were brought into existence on Day Five, and land animals and humanity were brought into existence on Day Six. From the inauguration of existence, onward, it has been apparent that life needs water to carry on.

Thus, when we pray for rain, we implicitly pray, as well, for the life-giving water that fosters our fruit trees and fields, for the heavenly kiss that greens our livestock's pastures, and for that precious liquid that elevates the waterways where our fish breed. We ask for rain since birds rely on precipitation, as do animals, and as do we.

Rabbi Yoseph Y. Jacobson wrote in "Souls in the Rain," "[w]hat is rain? In the midst of intimacy between heaven and earth, procreative drops from heaven are absorbed, fertilized and nurtured by mother-earth, which in time will give birth to its botanical children."[11] In short, no rain means no life. No heavenly water means no Earthly survival.

---

11. Yoseph Y. Jacobson. "Souls in the Rain." *Chabad.org.* http://www.chabad.org/library/article_cdo/aid/2557/jewish/Souls-in-the-Rain.htm.

Some mystics point out that the quality of rain depends on the quality, i.e. on the relative goodness, of our actions. In requesting heavenly waters, we evoke the merit of the Avot, as well as of Moshe, of Aaron, and of Yoseph. Rabbi Joel Padowitz explains in "The 7 Ushpizin Guests," that "Abraham represents love and kindness, Isaac represents restraint and personal strength, Jacob represents beauty and truth, Moses represents eternality and dominance through Torah, Aaron represents empathy and receptivity to divine splendor, [and] Joseph represents holiness and the spiritual foundation."[12] In other words, we ask Hashem to consider our merits, and to reward us, in turn, with rain.

Other sages say that rain derives from supernal sources and is of various types. Some kinds of water, for instance, are good for trees, whereas other types are good for vegetables. Rabbi Nathan Schapira states in "The Rains of Israel"[13] that some plants need "male waters," i.e. rain, and that other green growth can get by with "female waters," moisture from below, from seas, lakes and rivers.

Interestingly, "female waters" are sustained by "male waters." When it rains, for instance, in the Upper Galilee and in the Golan Heights, the flow of the Jordan River increases. Subsequently, the water level of the Kinneret, Israel's largest fresh water source, increases.

When, in contrast, the Kinneret's water level drops, we Israelis are forced to rely progressively more on desalinized water, on wastewater and on greywater. Desalinized water is often replete with bromides, that is, with seawater compounds. Wastewater, i.e. sewage water, can contain blackwater (human waste), manufacturing liquids, chemical-laden agricultural drainage, and other undesirable components. As per greywater, Amit Gross, et. al. write in "Environmental Impact and Health Risks Associated with Greywater Irrigation: A Case Study," that "greywater may be of similar [low] quality to wastewater in several parameters such as BOD and faecal coliforms. For some other variables

12. Rabbi Joel Padowitz. "The 7 Ushpizin Guests." *Aish.com.* http://www.aish.com/h/su/dits/48965711.html.

13. Rabbi Nathan Schapira. "The Rains of Israel." *Chabad.org.* http://www.chabad.org/kabbalah/article_cdo/aid/380819/jewish/The-Rains-of-Israel-102.htm.

such as boron and surfactants, greywater may even be of worse quality than wastewater."[14] Fresh water remains preferable to all available alternatives. We need rain because we need fresh water

Not surprisingly, Torah, which is the source of life at the most profound level, is equated to water. We beseech Hashem to open our souls to Torah. We beseech Him to send us Gishmei Bracha, the Divine blessing of rain, to gift us with the wet nourishment that falls on the right place, and G'shamim B'itam, the Divine blessing of rain that falls at the right time.

This wet week in Israel, we slosh through puddles and transport ourselves slowly. This wet week in Israel, we are blessed.

---

14. Amit Gross, et. al. "Environmental Impact and Health Risks Associated with Greywater Irrigation: A Case Study." *Researchgate.net*. Feb. 2005. https://www.researchgate.net/publication/7455989_Environmental_impact_and_health_risks_associated_with_greywater_irrigation A _case_study.

Faith

It's almost Shabbat, the time when we are temporarily blessed to add another dimension/a second soul. Soon, the holy air of the Holy Land will be infused with the chanting of prayers. Men will sing niggim. Women will lift their voices to bentshen lecht. Children will scurry in search of Shabbat treats, their joy expressed in all manner of shouting and sing-song.

In the morning, the birds, the lizards, and other indigenous creatures, too, will proclaim their part in this holy day. Few cars, at least in our neighborhood, will dirty up the audible world. Shabbat's hum will envelope us for twenty-five hours.

Until then, there are discordant noises with which to cope. First, a leader of a large and influential nation has sounded off about supporting our enemies and about leveling our homeland. Our foes literally, and figuratively, applauded that rhetoric and indicated that the war drums beneath their hands are only starting to beat. They'd only strive for peace, if, has v'shalom, we cease to exist.

Second, there is the hush of that political figure's nation. Few citizens have spoken up against the prejudice, the racism, or the hatred, which that leader's words wrought. Those persons speak of the importance of freedom, but make little movement to hush statements that work toward thwarting our nation's self-determination. In fact, for the entirety of our modern state's existence, there have been powerful distracters, who meant to contribute to our annihilation.

Third, there is the silence of the seventy nations of the Earth, that same lack of declaration that failed to ring out each time another monster voices a desire to exterminate our people. It is not merely the nay-sayers who are guilty of harming us, but also the individuals who remain calm in light of the possibility of our peril.

Fourth, there are the suppressed voices of our leaders. Those agents still fail to divorce themselves from currying international political favor, or to reunite themselves with the only True General.

There will soon be, IYH, the reverberation of silver trumpets heralding Moshiach and the patter of feet dancing in jubilation as the human king joins us. Then, as well, we will hear about the miracles that HaKadosh Baruchu has actualized to redeem us.

Until such a wonderful moment, though, it behooves us to point out the lack of friendly signals resonating around the globe and the great boom of ugly calls. We must attune ourselves to creating a better reality in the days to come. - Hannah

****

I really don't like explaining how to believe. I just had a *bagrout* in *emunah*. I don't really like being tested on ways of faith. I prefer to learn it and to live it, but not to have to write about it in full sentences. For that reason, I took extra classes on the subject, but elected to take only the most basic of the available tests.

There is, however, one thing I feel confident writing about; "good" vs. "for the good." One important thing about emunah is that everything is from Hashem. One should not believe that everything is good. Things are hard. Things are sad. One should, however, believe that everything is for the good, and as such, is part of a Divine Plan.

For me, for the most part, if I take time to think about the "big picture," I can often accept hard things that happen. I don't always understand why they happen, but when I realize they are from Hashem, they are a lot easier to deal with.

Some things, however, no matter how much I accept them, are never easy to deal with. One such thing is persecution. I have a hard time seeing my nation and land being persecuted by the world. It was hard for me to read

Obama's Egypt speech. It's also hard for me to read news about terrorist attacks, such as the death and injury caused by the ax murderer who killed in Bat Ayin. It's hard for me to listen to practice air raid sirens. It's hard for me to accept any and all imminent danger to me and to my people.

When I was younger, I used to imagine what it would be like to spend a day in a concentration camp. I wondered if I would be hungry, tired, or just complain about the work load. During the intifada, I started imagining living in a bomb shelter. I thought about food, about who would share my room, and about how I would go to the bathroom. I learned that it's easier to imagine a situation from the past or from across the world.

Now, Baruch Hashem, I live in the midst of an epic game of tug of war. Everyone wants Israel, and they want our land now. People of great power support the "other guys." Baruch Hashem, we have The Most Powerful on our side. Yet, I am still anxious.

I imagine the days of Moshiach. I wait for his coming. I want him to come sooner. Why must the birth pangs hurt so much? Nonetheless, I believe in complete faith in the coming of Moshiach, and even though he delays, I wait daily for his coming. – Rivka

G-d's Help Masked as "Accidents"

Protexia, one's social connections among people of power, is not always established on purpose. For instance, even when available, protexia need not to be used. Per Torah, it ought not to be used (see: Parsha Vayigash, on Yoseph allotting food to his family, during the famine, in accordance with his family's numbers, rather than in accordance with his relative place within the Egyptian hierarchy.)

It's not nice (as well as disallowed halachically) to take advantage of certain types of situations. Ultimately, all goings-on are machinations of The Boss's Will, even the establishment of "lucrative" social contacts. We remain unable to judge our own merit (or the lack thereof). We remain unable to assign reward or punishment for our actions, either as those consequences manifest in this world or as they will be manifested in The-World-to-Come. Therefore, the intentionality of protexia can be understood as being part of The Boss' domain.

BH, for that reason, I have been caused to meet many community leaders without having any initial inklings as to who they are. In each case, at the time of my introduction, I didn't need to know their social roles. What's more, although I now know their identities, that knowledge doesn't change my understanding of the situations in which we mutually participated (except to provide me with humorous anecdotes), nor does that information change future events, except for the fact that those people now number among the individuals my family looks upon as friends.

Once, for instance, when I invited for Shabbat lunch "a lonely old man," who I had met while walking home from shul, I had no idea "who he was." I didn't know, b'li ayin hara, that he was: blessed with a sizeable family, a rabbi of significant, and accustomed to helping large numbers (tens of thousands) of our people. I just saw a stranger walking by himself, near my home, around lunchtime. I felt bad that any Jew would miss the delights of a Shabbat table, so I invited him home.

As a result of my gesture (we Jews customarily make places for other Jews during Shabbat meals), I inadvertently endeared myself to this Rav. Even after my family made aliyah, from all the way across the ocean, he fondly teased me about my effort to "makiruv" him. Interestingly, I only meant to serve "an elderly loner" some fish, some soup, and some chicken alongside portions of singing, praying, and Dvrai Torah; I was not looking to meet an important community figure.

In another case, I was involved in learning with an older woman. My learning partner, BH, was a font of Torah. She was also personable. Silly me, I thought that, likewise, she was lonely/needed an outlet for her wisdom. When I joined the community in which she had long been a resident, I had incorrectly assumed that it was equally beneficial for us two moms to study together and that I was contributing something to our relationship. With the passage of time, I came to appreciate that I was the one receiving the gifts. I had had no idea about the uniqueness of the person with whom I was learning.

Imagine my amazement, when, after months of shared study, I was informed, by another member of our community, about the exceptionality of my partner. My Torah friend hardly needed a teaching opportunity. She hardly needed "an excuse" to get out of the house. My Torah friend was none other than the menachelet of an internationally known Bas Yaakov high school!

When I confronted her with my discovery of her extraordinariness, she asked, with her most mischievous smile, if that knowledge made me want to stop learning with her. I might be crazy, but I'm no fool. BH, we remained learning partners until nearly the time that my family moved to Israel.

During another occasion, this time after we aliyah, I wound up meeting a significant government official. Here, too, the person's remarkability was not originally clear to me; I thought I was communicating with a humble, neighborhood lady who spent her energies coordinating the delivery of home stuffs to the needy. Whereas my "contact" is humble and does help the poor, she is much more than a mere "neighborhood lady." Our initial conversation went something as follows;

Me: "So–and-So told me to call you to find an appropriate family to whom to donate the extra chairs, table, pots, clothing, and so forth I brought over on my lift."

She: "Do you know who I am?"

ME: "The lady who will help me actualize this chesed."

She: "Yes, but I am also the xyz of Jerusalem."

Me: "Okay (I didn't understand the government and didn't care. I just wanted to settle in the Holy Land), so after we bring this project to fruition, can you help me find more chesed opportunities? I'm new here and don't know where to help."

She: "You don't grasp what I'm saying, do you?"

Me: "Should I?"

She: "An xyz in Israel is similar to an xyq in the United States."

Me: "Okay."

She: "You're not from New York, are you?" (She then proceeded to explain to me the governance structure of New York City and to review for me the division of power of the American federal government. She finished her mini tutorial with a comparison of the Israeli and of the American governments and with an additional reference to her authority.)

Me: "Thanks (her explanation was succinct, but my mind remained on those pots and tunics). About those chesed projects…"

She: "If you need anything, here is my personal number and my assistant's number. Work on your Hebrew. Best of luck. Call me."

I promised to keep in touch, but refused to hang up until the details of the chesed project were smoothed out. I wanted to nest, not to noodle. Struggling Jews, not politics, were on my mind.

Yet, I am only human. After I finished arranging transportation (we filled two minivans with goods) for the drop-off to the family, which the politico had identified, and whom had crossed the Middle East on foot, taking with them only their lives, as well as a mother was both pregnant and suffering from a broken leg, I sat on a chair and thought about my conversation with the "neighborhood lady." Some things, such as her reference to "an assistant," didn't sit right. So, I reverted to a New World behavior; I googled her.

I found her name many, many times on the Internet. I grew frightened upon realizing just who I had been talking to; her community role is significant. I'm glad that I didn't initially grasp "just who" was my chesed partner.

Although the government official and I have not yet worked together on other chesed projects, we remain in communication. One Sukkot Mo'ed, my family and I visited her family. I'm happy to report that her husband is as lovely as is she.

Meanwhile, The Boss has made sure that I meet other government officials, other important rabbis, and the like, all under innocuous circumstances. I've given up trying to figure out people's "day jobs;" I just try to continue to concentrate on their middos and on my obligation to be kind to all members of Klal Yisrael.

Most recently, I interacted with a certain gal from a major publication. I ran into her because I had gone to a butcher who carries the only hecsher acceptable to certain of my Shabbat guests. Had I not been careful about my preparations for my company, I might not have reconnected with that member of the publishing world.

I don't understand the workings of the Universe. It's not in my job description to comprehend such things. My task is to be grateful for the human connections Hashem places in my life and to be careful not to exploit them.

A Springtime Letter to Friends

Dear Loved Ones,

There is bread in our house again. The dishes have been changed over from Pesach and the kids have returned to school. Even that child of mine, whose school placement was in question, has had that issue resolved. Additionally, I think I might have found a part-time job.

I've begun, again, to invite friends for Shabbat. My phone calls, this week, were to confirm guests for the next two months. What's more, I am signing up students for springtime writing workshops. I am likewise trying *not* to forget to count the Omer, that is, to acknowledge each of the forty-nine days between Passover and Shavuot.

Meanwhile, Older Dude is making noises about taking his bike out of storage and about not needing to wear a jacket anymore. That boy returns home from yeshiva, more often than not, sunburned from having spent his free periods playing American football. Think "gridiron," rather than "soccer," and think "tag" rather than "tackle" (there's only so much that youths can do in a paved, yeshiva courtyard.) Spring trips are within this young man's reach, too. His class, teacher strikes permitting, will be camping for a few days in some beautiful, uninhabited spot in the Galilee. Older Dude will come home dirty, tired, and hungry, but with days' worth of smiles. That child, who is just short of my height, BH, will also continue to grow.

As for Younger Dude, the more that he esteems the lengthening hours of sunlight, the more that he schemes about longer play dates with the neighbors' kids. He recently informed me that an unofficial tour of our community's playgrounds is long overdue and that he will continue to help me learn verbs, in Hebrew, as long as I continue to realize that such collaboration must take place after sunset. His precious hours of spring daylight oughtn't to be wasted being stranded inside by helping Mom overcome her language acquisition problems.

At the same time, Missy Younger pines to visit clothing stores. She will have to contend with waiting, though, since there will be no clothing shopping until after Shavuot. Plus, before the fiduciary floodgates open, she will have to inventory her earrings.

In the interim, the celebration of her becoming Bat Mitzvah will need planning. I want to buy her a pretty frock that she can also wear for the Yomim Noraim. Plus, if her grandparents, on both sides of the family, have their way, when they arrive in the Holy Land, they will be bringing her additional wearable gifts (it is useless to argue with grandparents whom possess documents verifying their unalienable right to spoil their grandchildren.) Until then, she will have to make due with "commonplace," entertainments such as interacting with the streams of young ladies visiting our home.

As for Missy Older, she's accompanying Computer Cowboy abroad. She hopes to raise money for a Jerusalem charity and to reunite with her old hevrusot. Missy Older hopes, too, to put closure on "this aliyah business." Classroom decorum, closed shoes instead of sandals, lack of conversational Hebrew, and other New World teenage "normalcies" will give her plenty to mull over on her trip.

Then, when she comes back to Israel, Missy Older will have to take her first bagrout, standardized examination in a core high school subject, to recommence braiding her local friends' hair, and to reengage classmates in pillow fights while on school trips. She might even start researching places where she can enroll, after high school, in sherut leumi, national service.

In the period in-between, other families we adore, too, will have returned to their state of "ordinary." There's at least one wedding on the horizon and the possibility of several more. Just a few days ago, too, a young friend, one of our B'not Bayit, brought her significant other *and* his parents to our home. Last week, I heard warm news, as well, about the forthcoming nuptials of a son of a friend, who lives in another Israeli city.

At the same time as the Pesach stupor crumbles, neighborhood invitations begin to flow. Gone are the days of friends' wall-to-wall children and grandchildren and returned are Shabbatot spent with local pals. One family invited us for a Shabbat meal *because* Computer Cowboy is going to be traveling; another family invited us for a different meal *because* Computer Cowboy will be returning. The first friend staunchly believes that absentee Shabbatot call for decreased kitchen duties. The second friend staunchly believes that reunion Shabbatot call for the same.

Weekday shiurim have started up, again, too. There are neighborhood classes and city classes in which to sit. The kids' tutoring, likewise, has fully resumed.

Additionally, I've returned to my Hebrew lessons. Two different sabra friends insisted that I visit them to practice letting go of English. Those ladies encourage me to struggle in all three tenses. One is a social worker. The other is a teacher. Because they have more patience than a room full of Jewish grandmothers, I obey their orders.

While we humans are preoccupied with springtime business, Hashem is stirring nature. Our mirpesset herbs are flowering. There is lemon balm for tea, rosemary for Shabbat chicken, and lavender for cakes. The mosquitoes have resumed their place among our local pests. The dumpster cats are again digging up our posies. Lizards, snails, and snakes have again been spotted.

We have been blessed with rain. We have seen the sun. We have experienced the wind. The land is refreshed, cleaned like our kitchen cabinets were prior to Pesach. My family's looking forward toward Lag B'Omer, to Shavuot, and to Tish B'Av (the last of which will be a feat day once Moshiach's here). All too quickly, the year will cycle.

Maybe, in the summer, we'll trek north, where Younger Dude is convinced grow wonderful blueberries, available for picking for two entire weeks. Maybe, we'll trek south (after all, one of Missy Younger's friends, IYH, will be celebrating her Bat Mitzvah in Efrat.) Maybe we'll bus to the east and float in the salty sea.

Soon, we'll be replacing Shabbat chicken soup with ices and lamenting the lack of sleep our littlest ones get on "late" Shabbat nights. Computer Cowboy will make more trips. I will write more essays. Life, IYH, will continue to be good.

As I look at the leaven that has come into our home (all of that bread remains incomprehensible to me) and at the increasingly expansive, porous blueness of the Jerusalem sky, I think about the warm months to come. Like the cooler ones, they, too, are good. May all of your days and nights be filled, in equal parts, with laughter and with light. May this spring and summer bring you only brachot.

The Holy Land

When, at the beginning of each day, we offer up morning prayers, Birkat HaShachar, we make a point of thanking Hashem for our breath, for our ability to walk, and for other physical basics. In some cases, we add personal thanks to the formal text. For my family, these extra gratitudes include our appreciation for being able to dwell in The Holy Land.

Whereas our ethnic cousins sound their culture through the loudspeakers mounted on their minarets, so, too, do our children's schools announce our presence in our land. Twinkling reverberations of voice or of instruments ring in one learning session after another. Additionally, Shabbat sirens sound from our hilltops at the requisite times. As well, the music of weddings wafts from catering halls.

In Israel, living the Torah means more than transversing our Daled Amot, our personal space. Life, here, also includes paying tribute to our forefathers at their keverim, celebrating our descendants, at their bnai mitzvot, plus drinking the water, eating the grain, and inhaling the air of this sanctified place. In Eretz Yisrael, living the Torah way of life means actively participating in local goings-on.

Unlike the other places, where we are temporarily encamped, Eretz Yisrael is home. Here, Am Yisrael is in sync with Hashem's continually established rhythms. Here, we feel the impact made by our deeds of loving kindness. Here, we can witness the impact our learning grants the world.

In this slip of Earth, circumscribed by the sea and by human enemies, we are able to visit the ruins of former Temples and to build the final one. In this slip of sky, bounded by human understanding and by other, linked realms, we are able to visit the ruins of our former blessings and to restore the final, absolute one.

When my family made aliyah, it was simultaneously to a modern state and to an ancient path. Our elevation forced us, as it does all comers, to choose between comfort and more important forms of status.

It is not simply that this land of Judea and of Samaria, of the Negev, and of the Golan, is a geography in which, a month before Sukkot, every hardware store offers frames for palm branches. It is not simply that bakeries in this land, a month before Hanukah, feature doughnuts, or that every two shekel shop, a month before Purim, offers baskets, candies, cookies, and liquors, or, immediately after Purim, offer soaps, buckets, andbrooms. Moreso, it is that here, in this juncture between worlds, Shabbat, the promise between the Almighty and His followers, is held as the most precious jewel. Here, in this juncture between worlds, the promise keepers, our Jewish children, are touted as precious.

There is actual wonder that detonates Israel's sands, pure miracles that drip through Israel's pipes, and genuine marvels that grow in every Israeli apartment. It ought not to be a wonder that dwelling here is so very good.
- Hannah

****

I find my Israeli friends funny when they try to sing English songs. I know I must sound equally amusing when I sing in Hebrew, yet their singing in English songs makes me laugh. One of their favorite songs is "Hakuna Matata," a tune from *The Lion King*. I don't know if my friends completely understand what they are singing, but I find that song fitting to Israeli culture and emblematic as to why I love this state.

"Hakuna Matata" means "what a wonderful phrase, Hakuna Matata, ain't no passing craze. It means no worries for the rest of our days…" Similarly, living in Israel means knowing that everything is going to be ok. Living here is about living in the moment, and not worrying about things that can't be changed. It's about loving life.

Living in Israel means taking public buses everywhere. I didn't always like taking a bus to school; the bus that travels closest to my school is "separated;" the boys sit in the front and the girls in the back. Over time, though, I have learned the difference between "separated" and "segregated" and have begun to appreciate why "separated" bus lines thrive here. In Israel, after all, taking a bus means helping women load strollers through bus doors and holding strangers' babies while those babies' mothers pay for their seats.

Likewise, missing a bus means having to pray while traveling. I don't like praying on a bus, but I have done so plenty of times, and I am never the only one doing so. Here, if you sway and mumble to yourself on a bus, bystanders don't accuse you of being drunk; they understand that you are davening. Further, in Israel, on Fridays, when you get off of a bus, the drivers wish you "Shabbat Shalom," a Good Sabbath.

Beyond commuting, living in Israel means dealing with Israeli shopkeepers. When I go clothing shopping, the storekeepers are not afraid to tell me when things don't look good on me. Granted, they will almost always offer a more expensive alternative to what I've picked out, but I've come to appreciate their Israeli frankness. If the store I'm in doesn't carry what I'm looking for, those same clerks will direct me to one that does. Shopping in Israel means talking to the other customers and learning their stories, too. It means the checkout girl will interrupt you with her own life story before you have finished yours, and that the lady behind you in line will also offer unsolicited advice.

In addition, living in Israel means going to an Israeli school. School in Israel can consist of more free periods than actual classes, and more field trips to university labs than time spent learning in your high school building. My Israeli high school experience was in no way what I expected, but I loved every minute of it.

What's more, living in Israel means embracing life. It means that everyone knows they are fortunate to be alive; since everyone, here, knows people who were murdered.

In spite of such large amounts of tragedy, Israelis are happy. We try to live every minute to its fullest. We don't waste time dwelling on things that cannot be changed.

In sum, living in Israel means living happy. I smile when I miss the bus, when I give up my seat to the lady with three kids, or when I help another woman with her stroller. I smile to the guard when I get to school late and I get a smile from the teacher who kicks me out of her class for my tardiness. I smile at the falafel store owners who are shocked at the amount of spice I can tolerate and at the shopkeepers who tell me I look fat. I smile because I live in Israel. I smile because I am home. Hakuna Matata. - Rivka

Let's Not Forget the Kedusha

In two different publications, I read about the imminent construction of high rise office and apartment buildings at the entrance to our blessed metropolis, near where that yet dysfunctional piece of expensive sculpture, The String Bridge, currently sits. Government officials are happy with those new plans, as are businessmen.

Those same reports maintain, though, that some of "us little people" are displeased with those goings-on (no "persons of importance," i.e. journalists, though, thought to *directly* solicit our opinions.) "Our" discontent was presented as inconsequential in that and in other, related matters. In fact, the newspapers presented "our" feelings as mostly supportive; after all, "we members of the masses" willingly continue to provide, via our taxes, the materials for such monuments. As a result, our overseers won't stop erecting those hewn testimonials. Our municipal administrators view "our" position, on preserving the holy nature of our city, as, at most, trifling.

Those persons in charge consider that "our" ilk cares so little about Jerusalem, specifically, and about Israel, in general, that soon "our" type will forfeit, altogether, our right to make aliyah, or will forfeit, in the least, upon arrival, any efforts to protect Jerusalem's sanctity. Those civic masters assume that "our" type remains content with just getting here. They deem that we hold back from applying ourselves to necessary civic work and that we have the tendency to gaze at our nation's ruble rather than to participate in her rebuilding. They do not know "us."

Sure, our leaders are correct in noticing that we are fonder of Tzionite music than we are of Tzionite duties. It's always been easier to celebration the holy quality of this sacred realm than to defend it. Thus, in noting our moaning that we cannot "finish the work," those supervisors necessarily view us as passive sorts who accept the gifts of the land, but who hesitate to champion her. They do not grasp our depths.

We transfer our "music," our respect for this realm's sanctity, to our friends. We share that music's infectious nature at Sma'achot, and write about how and why Israel's holiness inspires us. Sometimes, we are willing to surrender our comfort in order to continue dwelling here. Sometimes, we recall that our land is acquired through challenges, the utmost of which are often bitter or personal. Sometimes, we recognize: that tests are stairways to holiness, that we can elect to embrace our difficulties with joy, and that gracious living elevates us. Sometimes, we retain our appreciation that everything that occurs is meant to favorably shape us.

One day, our governing parties will see that our small voices place commerce after sensitivity, that we minions have long been nay-saying grandiosity in the quiet of our homes, and that we "others" have decided, "suddenly" to oppose obscenities in the forum of the streets. When, at last, "we insignificant sorts" begin to safeguard our city's precious soul, our would-be chiefs will come to understand that the only homages, which The Jewish People support, are the ones to Hashem. — Hannah

****

One of my favorite summer pastimes is tourist watching. My friends and I sit in the pedestrian mall, Ben Yehudah, and watch the tourists. I don't know what the tourists think of Israeli teens filling that space, but I enjoy filling it. For the cost of a slurpie, I manage to get a tan, some entertainment, and lots of perspective.

I love to see how the tourists go gaga over anything written in Hebrew and how the tourists seem certain that any building made out of Jerusalem stone must be from the Old City. Also, it's great to see tourists donate generously to the needy on the street. I like to listen to their conversations about the Kotel and The City of David. I watch them feel awe for Jerusalem. I feel jealous.

I've lost that awe. I no longer look at Jerusalem as the holiest city in the world, but as my home. There is nothing wrong with feeling that Jerusalem is home, but there is something very wrong in forgetting that my home is the Holy City.

When I take Jerusalem for granted, I forget that this place, where I am fortunate to live, is more than an open air shuk and more than a great bus network. I forget that it contains The Western Wall, the location for the future Temple. I forget that every religion wants to call this city their own. I forget that only in Israel do we hear the priestly blessing every Shabbat. I forget my good fortune.

Every now and then, I come to my senses. I remember people died trying to live the life I live freely. At those times, I go to the Kotel more often, and pray with more intensity. Those times are too infrequent. I've become comfortable with my life. I don't feel that I'm in Jerusalem, and I don't feel that I miss the Temple.

Meanwhile, I still encourage everyone who lives in Israel, or who is visiting the Jewish Nation, to remember the significance of the Holy City. I silently shout out to them to be aware of how blessed they are to be here.

Sure, the tourists are annoying, but I have a lot to learn from them. It's time that I wake up and join them in embracing Jerusalem's kedusha. – Rivka

Good Home Beautiful

Like other Jews, the world over, when the members of my family open their eyes, each morning, they thank The Creator for restoring them to life. Unlike most of the rest of the Klal, to date, my family is able, as well, b'ayin tova, to say "thank-you" for allowing them to wake up in Jerusalem.

Living in the Holy City ought not to be taken for granted. Whereas my kin and I have merited to live in, or to visit commerce centers as well as to live in, or to visit places where Hashem's nature-manifested miracles are palpable, none of those other locations are as valuable as is this spot, where Heaven and Earth kiss.

It is undeniable that the Alps, for instance, are a tacit expression of The Boss's glory. Few other districts on this planet are as compelling in their grandeur as are those famous peaks. Analogously, the Pacific Ocean, especially at sunset, is a place of innate majesty.

If my family was wowed by material considerations, then New York City would rank among unrivaled places for its ability to represent and to provide for many types of people. That glass and concrete maze is home to: financial and art centers, fashion and culinary innovations, and many Jews. Nonetheless, the Big Apple, like the Hollywood-influenced city of Los Angeles, and like the formerly industrial cities of Detroit and Pittsburgh, lacks heightened holiness.

Similarly, I appreciate the countryside around Paris and the waterways that enhance life south of Zürich. It is certainly the case that the history of Montreal is long and interesting. No city in North America, in Europe, or elsewhere on the globe, though, offers the spiritual goodness that can be inhaled in Jerusalem.

Here, whether in upscale neighborhoods, or in more modest urban districts, sanctity pervades the most minute daily experiences. While our black-hatted neighbors fight on the behalf of our entire people, by sharpening their prayers and loading up on Torah knowledge, our bare-headed friends make sure that kids cross the street safely and that lost tourists receive no further misdirection. With words and deeds, our collective knits a fabric of devotion and of goodness.

My husband, children and I appreciate the redwoods of Northern California and the hetaeras of birch in Vermont. We're charmed by the shells swept up along Atlantic Ocean beaches and by the craggy shores of the Scottish coast. Were we to visit Victory City in Hong Kong, or Wellington, New Zealand, it is likely that we would be impressed by those cities' stunning harbors, too. Yet, my family would not trade even a minute of Jerusalem's crazed intersections or questionable panhandlers for a single forest vista or for one more access road to urban wonder.

By dint of Hashem's Kindness, we have found our way to the Center of the universe. Here, every dwelling is a good home and every dwelling is beautiful. - Hannah

****

Living quarters seem to come up a lot in fairy tales. There is the candy cottage from Hansel and Gretel, the tower where Rapunzel was held captive, the dirty shack that Snow White was always cleaning for the seven dwarves, and the little old lady who lived in a shoe. All of those houses played large roles in their stories.

Take the tower, for example. If Rapunzel had lived in a walk-in apartment, she would have had nowhere to lower her hair and her prince would never have had to scale a wall or to use her locks as support to take her away to "happily ever after." If the witch's house was built in the same fashion as were the three little pigs' homes, Hansel and Gretel would never have been tempted to eat her roof. Instead, they would have learned how to trap and skin rabbits, or at least how to pick berries. Had the dwarves lived in a hotel, maid service would have picked up after them and security would have kept out the Evil Stepmother. Houses are important.

It's not only in stories that dwellings are significance. My house, too, is important; I am lucky to live in Jerusalem. While I can't eat my walls when I get hungry in the middle of the night since they are made of Jerusalem stone, they are a strong representation of where I am. Even though my room is hardly as clean as it might be if I had a live-in princess to tidy things up, I don't miss the company of seven boys; my two brothers are plenty.

On the other hand, like Rapunzel, I have dreams that could take place just outside of my window. The difference between me and her is that all I have to do is walk out my front door to be in the best place in the world. She had to make a pulley system out of her hair.

There is nowhere in the world like Jerusalem. Nowhere else can I wish the bus drivers "Shabbat Shalom" on Fridays and know that they understand me. There is nowhere else with a kosher falafel stand on every corner. In no other place is it possible to look at the street on Yom Kippur and see no cars, save for police vehicles.

I am very grateful that I have been given the chance to grow up in such a holy place. I am certain that where I live is much more than just a house; it's a home. - Rivka

The Social Milieu of Israel

Royalty

Tonight, Thank-G-d, I sat among royalty. I'm not quite sure as to which tribe those princes and princesses belong, but I am quite certain that I was graced to join with and to observe the words and deeds of sovereigns.

In harmony with Jewish law, rulers are no so much our masters, though we are expected to yield to and pray for them, as they are our people's servants. More specifically, our people's most elevated guides, at the best of times, are modest souls, who, in their awe of G-d, pattern for us means to act in our relationships to Him and to each other. They perform kindnesses, both overt and surreptitious, and sacrifice personal comfort in order to pull themselves and the rest of us to higher levels.

Tonight, I was torn between breathing in/infusing myself with the palpable decency of those special individuals and running to emulate them. The remarkable qualities of the evening included not only the excellence of the family's attributes, which was their guests' gift to receive, but also the depth, among the family's generations, in which those traits were readily perceivable.

I was conflicted between hugging the sisters of the hostess, kissing her mother and doting over her daughters and daughters-in-law. It would have taken inhuman sentiment not to feel authentic affection toward her granddaughters, as well.

After kissing a fairly recently coined bride, hugging that bride's aunt, and giving over warm words to that aunt's sister, I turned my attention to the other people in the room. The host's quiet wisdom has long drawn students and colleagues, all versed in Torah, all humbly busy helping our community.

I smiled seeing his sons, his sons-in-law, his grandsons, and his friends. I beamed even more when he gave over words of Torah and when his younger boy, the celebrant, who was a newly recognized Bar Mitzvah, spoke holiness, on the occasion of having completed the study of an admirable amount of Torah commentary.

Beyond the people, past the windows of the room, where the rite was unfolding, further than the guitar music and the sound emanating from the blessings recited around the words of Torah, around the meal, and throughout the evening, shone the ancient stones of the Kotel. In echo, in answer, and in vocal undulations, which began, at the Kotel, where the party had yet to begin, the new month's prayers of the faithful wafted – they traveled from the holiest place on Earth to the holy gathering in the room, where we sat, danced, and praised G-d, a few stories above.

It is not so much that the small children glistened in hues of sunglow and of pale gold (if I could capture in paint the energy radiating from their neshemot, I would use those colors.) nor was it the almost tangible goodness of the friends of the Bar Mitzvah boy's siblings that fill the shared space with their abundant goodness. Rather, it was the movement toward fulfillment, by the uncrowned heads of a Torah way of life that lifted us higher and higher.

On balance, every zenith is finite. Sometime before the party was completely over, my husband and I made our way down the hill toward our people's most precious site, intending to pray before we once more interacted with our own children.

After I finished my tefillot, I looked up. Even the shrubbery that grows from the Kotel's crevices was showing love; the plants were in bloom. I have never before seen their brilliant, tiny flowers.

As I backed out, in reverence, from the women's section, I discovered that I had been moving away in tandem with the footfall of a friend. That wonderful woman, who I hadn't seen while I was busied with prayers, too, had gone up to the Kotel by coming down the stairs from the seudah.

When we at last reached the space where it is permitted to turn our backs on the place of great holiness, when we again faced up the hill, where, on that particular night, goodness continued to be modeled, my friend embraced me. She whispered words with which I agreed; we guests were blessed to join the celebration of a family of true leaders.

Sweet Seudah Bar Mitzvah

Life before Pesach is not just about tidying up; life before Pesach is also about joy, which, per se, can be found in ordinary, but nonetheless elevated, events such as watching the sun rise over the hills of Jerusalem or sharing Shabbat with a dear friend, her children, and her grandchildren. Joy can be found, too, in specific events, such as festive meals associated with lifecycle moments. Another Bar Mitzvah, which Computer Cowboy and I recently merited to attend, fit this latter category.

To begin with, the invitation to that seudah was especially beautiful. The paper, which beckoned to us, was not distinct because of its carefully crafted placement of type or because of the quality of fibers upon which it was printed (although both of those properties were noteworthy for the invitation was more aesthetic than most), but because at the bottom of that celebration's note special kavod was given to the Bar Mitzvah boy's grandparents.

At the party, itself, even the photographer, either through the hosts' instructions, or through his own astuteness, made sure to capture the celebrant's Saba and Safta. He took posed shots of the grandparents as well as casual pictures. He made certain that the significant presence of the family's elders would be a permanent reference to the happy event.

As for the grandparents, I can attest that the grandma presided graciously over a table on the women's side of the mechitzah. That sweet and wise New York matron lovingly accepted kind words about her family while concurrently engaging guests, many of whom were strangers to her. I wasn't directly privy to the goings-on on the other side of the room, but, per my husband's report, the grandpa was every bit as gracious as was the grandma.

During the meal, there was much delight served beyond the tasteful buffet. More specifically, there were old friends and new acquaintances with whom to talk. I, for one, tasted happiness each time that guests entered and greeted the Bar Mitzvah boy's mom. I was completely satisfied by the hugs and smiles.

It was wonderful, as well, to hear the words of Torah given over by the Bar Mitzvah boy. We moms nodded and beamed as we listened to his well-articulated, clearly parsed speech. It's a frank pleasure to witness youth authentically embracing the Torah way of life.

Other forms of enjoyment that this seudah called into existence included: sharing pictures of grown children and grandchildren, catching up on friends' professional goings-on, and meeting an adorable elementary-aged little girl. Small kindnesses, too, contributed scrumptious moments to the festive night.

Eventually, though, I had to abandon all of those lovely talks of shidduchim, of shiurim, of coffee klatches, and of stores featuring good prices on Pesach goods. I had to stop consuming those entirely agreeable interpersonal morsels because I had to go home. My better half, who knew no one on his side of the divider, had more than gallantly participated in a party to which his only claims to belonging were his relationship to me and his Jewish birthright.

Well-sated, I said good night to the sweet school girl who had declared me a "good" grownup for having participated in a wild variant of handshakes and related greetings (I understood the knuckles pressed together and the high fives, but lost the nuance of some of her other means of connecting her mitts with mine) and to the easy leisure with which my new acquaintances spoke. I hugged and kissed known friends good night, too.

On route home, Computer Cowboy and I compared notes. His evening had been pleasant. In fact, he had only nice things to say about the men with whom he had spoken and about the convenience of being able to daven Ma'ariv while at the party. Further, the man of my life admitted that he never tires of beholding new beginnings.

At the next traffic light, however, my lassoer of stray code yawned. He looked at me with those eyes I still find irresistible even after all of our shared decades (b'li ayin hara), and said, softly, that his night would best be culminated with a bit of sleep.

Partying, Israeli-Style

My family, Baruch Hashem, has been partying. Our lives have been filled, b'li ayin hara, with Chatanot, Sheva Brachot, Seudot Bnai Mitzvah, Brit Milot, and even a Hanukkah HaClinic (friends opened up a new, private, medical facility.) We have been enjoying these events partially because each life is a treasure whose markers are to be cherished, and partially because such goings-on help my family remain cognizant of the relative significance of our days and nights (though, as my *Kohelet* teacher reminds me, our negative experiences, too, lend perspective.)

Whereas "regular" days are wondrous, especially if they are lived in Jerusalem, holidays arrive with separate expectations. That is, on "regular" days, we presume to: get our kids ready for school, go to work, prepare meals, enforce bedtime, etc., but on holidays, we presume to: say additional prayers, attend to additional laws, and partake in additional rituals. Sma'achot are that much more singular as they exist irregularly and as they make atypical prospects available to us.

The essence of sma'achot, unlike the essence of regular days, and to some degree, unlike the essence of holidays, is not universals, but instances. We can and ought to take advantage of happy instances. We're well advised to do so via autopoietic communication.

Autopoietic communication is: communication created on/by its own merit, communication that constitutes its own environment, and communication that self-referentially constructs reality. This type of communication can be exemplified by the sentence, "I knight you." In contrast, nonautopoietic communication is: communication created per social standards, communication which is a component of its environment, and communication which frames reality. This type of communication can be exemplified by the sentence, "I love that knight."

We establish and define our discrete selves via autopoietic communication. We establish and define our social selves via nonautopoietic communication. Both types of discourse are existential and imperative.

Whereas we are social creatures by nature/halacha (most of my Chassidishe friend can explain how the concepts of "Creation" and of "Divine Law" are actually a single impulse), we are simultaneously unique specks. Although most of our life experiences develop our nonautopoietic communication, select experiences, such as sma'achot, develop our personal distinctions.

For instance, a young person, who hopes to meet his or her bashert, is more likely to have the opportunity to interact with just the right fresh face at a wedding than at Aunt Sophie's Shabbat table. Perhaps, that is why some hosts of chatanot set aside special seating for friends of the bride and groom. Ostensibly, this segregation takes place so food is not wasted on dancing feet. Actually, this segregation takes place so food is not wasted on gazing eyes. Whether chatanot-attending youths are literally skipping, juggling, weaving, and otherwise physically reaching to where souls are meant to ascend, or are figuratively skipping, juggling, weaving and otherwise emotionally reaching to where souls are meant to ascend, chatanot-attending youths take advantage of sma'achot's exceptional nature to become elevated.

Similarly, business people might get introduced to Uncle Joseph's neighbor's law partner when visiting Uncle Jo for Pesach, but those businesspeople won't be able to talk to that law partner about work-related matters during the Seder. At a Seudah Bar Mitzvah, on the other hand, excepting the time devoted to brachot, to Dvrai Torah, to davening, and to other prescribed activities, it is entirely possible for those businesspeople to talk to that partner about legal issues or about job leads that partner might have for their children. Milestone-marking celebrations contain many junctures during which the affirming of individual identities can supersede the validation of social roles.

Analogously, although we Israelis welcome frank direction from our dearest companions, it is usually during special occasions, that is, during the times when we reunite with loved ones from places geographically or temporally distant from our habitulized points, that we glean our most exacting perspectives on our lives. It is not so much that our foreign-based families or seldom seen friends have a more refined view than do our regular buddies, as it is that folk uninvolved in our daily lives see us from fresh angles. More exactly, people removed from our regular vectors can more readily spot our successes, and, consequently, can more efficiently bolster us, as well as can more readily notice our shortcomings, and, consequently, can, more effectively give us mussar, than can our usual companions. Sma'achot are incomparable in their ability to create the conditions for such insights.

Not only do sma'achot help us gain commentary on our lives, but sma'achot also enable us to add to our internal points of view. Through celebrations, we can more readily refer to, remember, and learn from our deepest referents, i.e. from links to our most fundamental sensations and experiences than we can through mundanities.

The music played at a wedding, for example, might call to mind one's own initiation of a lifelong union. Seeing a friend in tulle and lace, for instance, might stir up childhood memories of similar occasions (when my sister and I were three, and six, respectively, we were the reigning princesses at the nuptials of one of our second cousins. Sis' dress was a fantasy of pink strata and mine was a pale turquoise dream.) Smelling another guest's perfume might help us reminiscence about bringing our own diaper-wrapped sweetums to happy times (it's tough for mothers to leave nurslings at home.)

Regardless of whether the enhancement comes from without or from within, sma'achot are a pleasure. It is not merely the reality of yeshiva boys walking hand in hand, or the actuality of seminary girls hugging each other, that gives off warm feelings. It is not just the altitude to which we are carried by oldsters' playing acoustical guitars and drums that infuses delight into our lives. It is not only the costumed waitstaff, the twinkling lights, or the wash of contentment on friends' faces that reverberates goodness in our souls. Likewise, it is not solely the late hour of most of these happy events that elicits our mental wooziness and makes us more inclined to smile.

Rather, it is the fact of layers of self that are added on, beyond our normal everyday experiences, that makes us giddy at life junctures. Despite the truth that the manifold manifestations of ruach cannot be delineated into neat units for the purpose of analysis, the *joi de vivre* that is attendant to sma'achot can and ought to be appreciated for its self-restorative potency. We linger at happy events, drink one more demitasse of espresso, take one more selfie with an honored celebrant, and hug friends and family again and again. We stay so as to hold on to the heightened sensibilities that sma'achot evoke

Street Smarts

"They're going to repossess our house!" he yelled, his face the color of raw hamburger.

"Don't matter if I'm dead," she sighed, her face the hue of seagull droppings.

She pressed the button on their car phone that terminated his response and then switched on the CD she had inserted the night before. Both their financial crisis and her health problems needed immediate attention.

In tending to him, to her thoughts about their challenges, and to the music, she had missed the sign, which informed her that her path went into a literally hostile village. Many moments later, she noticed the women with head scarves and the turban-crowned men.

She looked for a round-about, for a break in the highway at which to make a U-turn, or for some other means to reverse her choice. No such opportunities existed; she was committed to a long, one-way street.

Kilometers later, at a traffic light, she spun herself back toward the direction of safety. When stopped for the red light, she had seen smileless teens approach her vehicle. A friend's car had been totaled the previous week by a similar "welcoming committee."

That friend was driving home in the company of an armed husband, an armed brother-in-law and a possibly armed sister-in-law. That family's community is surrounded by the settlements of unfriendly others, by people who had broken all of the road's street lamps and who had left a cement truck parked at the end of one of its rural bends.

That friend, as the trappers had hoped, had crashed head-on into the others' truck. That friend had crushed her car entirely, but, had somehow, miraculously, not injured herself or her passengers. Stunned, that friend and her family had stumbled out of their auto and had immediately called the army for help.

While waiting for backup, that friend and her family had walked quickly away from the wreck. They had been trailed by the same locals who had placed the truck in the road. That friend and her loved ones had nearly reached their community when the others closed in. In desperation, the husband and the brother-in-law fired into the crowd. The would-be attackers dispersed.

Later, representatives of the army, who belatedly appeared at that friend's village, mentioned something about other vehicles, about other civilians being preyed upon at that turn in the road, and about the army's awareness that certain street lamps were not functioning. However, by the time that those army representatives had escorted the friend's husband and the brother-in-law back to that scene, neither her destroyed car nor the felonious truck was in sight.

Understandably, that friend was hysterical for a week. She remained sleepless for a month.

The woman, whose anger got her lost in an inhospitable community, reflected on her friend's tale as she drove through the streets of the others. She wondered if urban violence emulated countryside brutality. When, at last, she reached the artery, from which she had mistakenly turned, she again exhaled.

A bit thereafter, the woman pushed the button that rolled down her windows. She did not again press "play," on her music panel. Instead, she pulled off of the road to pray gratitudes. There are more immediately challenges than debt or bad health.

Arab Men

Arab men, whose Hebrew betters mine by generations, sit roadside smoking cheap cigarettes. They alternate waving hands and rocks. I accelerate just a little.

The road I travel to teach EFL at a university is frequented by all sorts; those with yellow license plates and those with white. Sometimes, sloppy trucks, whose chickens or crates of watermelon threaten to create hazards, pass without anyone's official placard.

Months ago, I took a holiday on a beautiful mountain. Although my guestroom's walls were a montage of water marks, of mold, and of chipping plaster, the dining room was resplendent with beautiful food and with beautiful service. In the midst of the emerald cucumbers, the white goat cheese, the slim, pink slices of salmon and the bright red tomatoes, I paused to consider that the waiters, ever quick to refill glasses or to top off shared platters, had an homegrown accent.

Their smiles and hair were doppelgangers to those of my kin, but their articulated vowels and consonants differed. I watched a bit and noticed, as well, that their gestures were not those of my nation.

My framesmith, too, comes from that other tribe. With skills more and more frequently relegated to nostalgia, he surrounds the colors and textures of my paintings and prints with enhancing wood and plaster. Although he is expert at his work, his bosses pay him a small wage; there exists a tiered system.

When I buy vegetables, the shopkeeper and his helpers assist me in discerning among their many heaps; they understand that I purchase only fruits and greens approved by specific assemblies. If I reach for the "wrong" cherries or for an "incorrect" head of lettuce, these men gently redirect me to the comestibles that my family eats.

And yet, during my village's times of quiet prayer and of other reverence, those same cousins shoot fireworks. They also blast their public address system late at night. Those ethnic relatives find no fault in chopping down our mutual forests or in constructing houses, on lands for which my brothers paid steep mortgages or for which they bled to protect.

In our land of sun and heat, there is more that bewilders me than the bray of donkeys or the goings-on in the open air markets. Specifically, I have yet to fully comprehend my relationship to Arab men.

The Olive Pickers

First, the stabbing, thereafter, the fruits.

I was sickened to learn that a friend's son was nearly killed a few weeks ago by an unwelcomed comer, a dweller from a nearby, TV dish-studded, car filled, McMansion "refugee camp." That malevolent had brought his misshapen knife to realize the political fantasies of his twisted mind. The actualization of his mentations meant plunging his blade into an innocent, whom that evil being had never met, and whom he would have as easily exchanged, per his creed, for any other harmless Jew.

BH, our young man is recovering.

Even had the trespasser not had murder on his mind, I would have been repulsed, a short time later, i.e. a few days before this essay was written, when I witnessed his wicked cohorts pulling ripe sustenance from a tree sprouting in the center of my community. Those olive pickers were stealing my people's harvest.

Our ethnic cousins engage in dark deeds with impunity. They whine to the world about their intent to ask their philosophical comrades to withhold oil, if any amongst their crowd gets so much as frowned upon when engaging in shocking pursuits. They succeed to the extent that they consider themselves entitled, has v'shalom, to kill our babies in their cradles.

In the minds of those Semitic relatives of ours, their acting out is part of their international "growing up." Their choices are a "desirable" part of the propaganda with which they wash the media.

I think not.

I am tired of being told not to bother to call Jerusalem's municipal police when loss is impending or when loss has occurred. I am tired of being told that if I engage the IDF in reporting manslaughter, or in reporting attempts at atrocities, that my nation's protectors will deliberately overlook that slaughter, sometimes because of commands, and sometimes, for fear of being jailed for valiance.

It is time for the world to stop being held hostage by its energy appetite. What's more, it is time for Am Yisrael to stop compromising because of fear. "No" needs to be the beginning and the end of any communication given to depraved persons.

When I drive through my community, I do not want to see THEM. I do not want those criminals in *my* neighborhood as laborers. I do not want them in *my* parks, harvesting from *my* olive trees. I do not want them trying to kill *my* friends' children. I do not want them exempt from justice in this world (or in the world to come).

I as I write this essay, we are in Cheshvan. Next month is Kislev, the time of Chanukah. As Rabbi Yehudah Prero writes in "Chanukah and Olive Oil: Lessons in Devotion," "[t]he only plant that withstood the corruption that permeated the entire world …was the olive tree. It remained pure. It withstood the pressures to engage in the perverse behavior that was in vogue at the time. The olive remained faithful to the world order as G-d created it."[15] Therefore, it is especially vile to see defilers in my community, brazenly plucking my olives.

It is of no small coincidence that it is illegal to destroy olive trees and that this concept is allegedly "revered" even by those louts. Likewise, it is of no small coincidence that it is immoral for Jews to destroy fruit trees of any kind and that it is immoral for Jews to allow other nations to steal their geographic heritage whether our birthright is measured by a block of communities, by a yeshuv, by a lone farm, or by an individual specimen *aeuropaea*.

Yet, those abominable others proudly rape and murder our olive trees in the same way that they proudly rape and murder our sisters and brothers

---

15. Rabbi Yehudah Prero, "Chanukah and Olive Oil: Lessons in Devotion." *Torah.org.* https://torah.org/learning/yomtov-chanukah-5756-vol2no22/.

and in the same way that they continuously refresh their call for our loved ones' demise. In the world arena, Eretz Yisrael gets tossed on the heap as something cheap and disposable, that is, as a short-term, political convenience for the dollar, yen, and euro. Our Holy Land gets treated as no having no more value than the firewood filched from our sacred olive trees.

Too many "well intending" NGOs, including, but not limited to mass media and to "aid" organizations invoke the needs of their vaporous causes in order to rationale their attempts to destroy the Jewish people and to wreck more than havoc within our consecrated land. International and local government and quasigovernment organizations look the other way when dastardly events occur.

Most of us Israelis, olim, as well as families here for multiple generations, are normal folk. Whereas we might aspire to the heights of scholar warriors, in most cases, we fill our days and nights with washing dishes, with praying, with chasing children from Point A to Point B, with community service, with folding laundry, with paying very large chunks of our earnings to support our national and local infrastructures, with reserve duty, and with otherwise making time to sit down for a salad or for a hummus-filled pita. Sadly, also typical, is our growing, collective feeling of weariness.

We are tired of being cut down in body and land. Our ideas are vital to us and to the nations, as a whole. Our legacy was given to us by our Creator.

No good can come, either to us, or to the entire globe, from ignoring, or from indirectly or directly abating attackers, who meditatively seek and conscientiously work to destroy our sons and daughters and to annihilate our fauna and flora. No good can come, either, to us, or to the entire globe, from ignoring, or from indirectly or directly abating, attackers, who meditatively seek and conscientiously work to visit these iniquities upon us while insisting on freedom from harm. Until that span when retribution, of an unearthly sort, occurs, we will suffer. The world's "olive pickers" must be caused to stop culling our wost precious harvests.

Dissatisfaction with Synthetics

As I restore order to my closet, during the days following my family's massive, post-holiday laundering, that is, as I again fold piles of shirts and of skirts, I consider the per cent of synthetic products in my piles, which were made in Israel. When I made aliyah, I promised myself I would only invest in lasting purchases, yet, these days, I find myself a willing consumer of inferior creations. I wonder why we Israelis make do with junk goods and why we are willing to pay absurd prices for them.

Granted, ours is an island economy, i.e. is a society cut off, on all sides, from friendly trading partners. Akin to inhabitants of lands surrounded by water, we are forced to consume merchandise that we would spurn in other circumstances. I am amazed, for instance, that so much of the locally available produce comes in cans, rather than in boxes of fresh or frozen stuff, given that we live in an agricultural wonderland. I am stunned, too, to discover that so much of the clothing offered to residents, here, uses manmade textiles despite the fact that our hills are full of sheep and our farms are full of cotton.

Not only does Israel export our best produce to North America and to Europe and our finest textiles to the Far East, to India, and to Turkey, but we, likewise, seemingly ship off our paramount sensibilities. As a population, we either rationalize that shoddy craftsmanship is sufficient for our needs, or we devote ourselves to longing for, that is, to drooling over, offerings advertised on the bandwidths of the convergent media.

If we were a nation that lacked natural resources or that lacked the talent to skillfully utilize our resources, it would make sense that we accepted cheap, Asian-sourced clothing, inexpensive, Russian wigs, and tins of fish from Oceania. However, we are a people blessed with intellect and creativity, and gifted with a land abundant in climates and in mineral-enhanced soil. Because of the composition of our dirt, our plants yield copiously and our milk cows yield the most milk in the world.[16] Nonetheless, we scramble to find certain vegetables in the shuk and we remain impoverished, relative to other nations, per the artisan dairy industry.

I'm not advocating that our farmers, our food chemists, our clothing designers or any of our related professionals concede fortune reaped from exporting goods or ideas. What I am espousing is that some portion of this nation's premium yields should stay home. Until such time, I will make due with folding piles of synthetic clothing and with cooking "Grade B" peppers.

16. Yuval Dror. "Udderly Marvelous Gina: Israel's Most Productive Cows." *Haaretz.* https://www.haaretz.com/udderly-marvelous-gina-israel-s-most-productive-cow-1.123444.

Apple-Scented Toilet Paper

I'm not a curmudgeon. I can still be surprised. I laugh at the fact of my astonishment, too. This week, for instance, Computer Cowboy brought home apple-scented toilet paper. When we both realized the specifics of the product (just how carefully do most people observe anything but the price of such goods), we snickered and guffawed.

Mind you, my man hates scents. Although, prior to meeting him, I was besotted with toilet water, with cologne, with perfume, and with all things sniffed at, I gave up my repertoire of "smelly" items in exchange for a steady dose of my husband.

Ours were scent-free candles. Ours were cent-free baby wipes. Ours is the home filled with scent-free household cleaning products.

It never occurred to my spouse (or to me, for that matter) to check to see if the goods with which we wipe were olfactorily altered. We have long held that the smells that issue from our water closet can no more be masked by perfumes than they can by aerosols. In our home, we long chanted, "open a window!" Unfortunately, our Israeli home's bathrooms lack this architectural feature.

Nonetheless, our noses (mouths and throats) understand basic human odor. Laboratory-produced scent is a useless camouflage against the messages received by the nerve cells in human membranes dedicated to the sense of smell. Expensive chemicals are rendered meaningless when met head-on by sharp organic stink. Artificial fragrance, at worse, irritates people exposed to such funk. At best, such fragrance is a misuse of crafted and of naturally occurring resources.

Even given the above, I suppose, on more careful reflection, that I ought not to have been astonished by the apple-scented toilet paper; wastefulness seems to be sanctioned by some of the local authorities. My favorite example of this phenomenon is the string bridge which is slowly and expensively rising near the entrance of holy Jerusalem.

Many pundits have had their say about this bridge. I'm not certain about just how many of them, though, focused their discourse on the structure's frivolity.

To be fair, I associate "frivolous" with "fun." When our children were small, we picnicked under the table, ate dinner on a blanket spread on the salon floor, or otherwise tweaked our dining routine to add light to our lives. During relevant Hagim, my family's been known, respectively: to run around in absurd costumes delivering beribboned baskets of sweets; to play musical matzah, i.e. to pass a napkin-wrapped half slice from lap to lap in an effort to keep the little ones from finding it; and to aid our rabbi in pouring branches, stems, petals, and more around the important parts of our Beit Knesset.

As per more personal celebrations, such as birthdays, my family can be counted on to be riotous. My clan takes seriously any license to party. During a certain offspring's recent celebration, and event best rubricked as between "bedlam"and "pandemonium," we supplied riotous boys with water balloons.

Although that particular party featured no: prearranged fire trucks (as did one of our parties a decade earlier – yes, the neighbors were worried), measuring of how many children can fit under a bunk bed while being timed by a stopwatch (occasionally we have to get creative to keep our guests happy), and no belly dance lessons (don't all middle-aged mamas discharge their menfolk from their home so that they and their gal pals can celebrate), that event was remarkable in its sporadic blurs of movement, which, per my jaded teens, were the vapor trails (think airplanes, not chemicals) and puddles left behind by our small guests. At least no one was hurt and everyone had fun.

Whereas party entertainments, holiday merriments, and child-centric feats of make-believe are expected to fulfill specific functions without worrying about being soundly based in reality, city infrastructures, on the other hand, must be neither derivative nor dependent. More to the point, bridges ought to be securely fastened to citizens' needs.

I'm not sure I can make this claim about the structure rising near Jerusalem's bus station. I'm supposing that any deficit, which exists in the bridge's reliability, exists because there are (literal and figurative) strings attached.

We Israelis, who bemoan our increasing poverty, our dearth of monies for schools, and our lack of budgetary dedication to soup kitchens and other means of feeding our poor, somehow seemed to have had enough money to direct large sums toward a structure which neither blends with the skyline (in Jerusalem, the streetscape necessarily must be colored by the golds and pinks of dolomitic limestone, i.e. by "Jerusalem stone"), nor is guaranteed to improve the life of the typical citizen (merchants and other backroom players aside, few locals care about the economics of, say, the pedestrian mall since Israelis shop wherever the best prices can be found.)

Basically, lots of tax revenue (more than 250 million NIS) has been taken from our pockets for a municipal project that may prove as superfluous as apple-scented toilet paper. Let's hope that the bridge doesn't prove to be worse. I can't help thinking about what would happen, if, G-d Forbid, that bridge fell during a war or a natural disaster.

That hunk of alloy weighs a lot. Special cranes and other greater-than-industrial-strength tools were shipped to Israel to build that structure and will be shipped back out when the project is completed.

If, after the contractors' toys are put away, has v'shalom, the bridge totters, even if no one is hurt, we will be left without a means of picking it back up or of clearing our streets of its gargantuan chunks. In such an event, not only would we have poured out our money to build an ineffectual colossus, but we would have to decant even more of our precious funds to clean it up. I, for one, am averse to flushing anything exotic down the communal commode.

I hope the string bridge remains merely ugly and wasteful. I know that when my family does something ugly and wasteful, like purchasing "enhanced" toilet tissue, there is an end to our loss; we are quickly able to use up our sorry purchase and to replace it with something more suitable. In contrast, I suspect that Jerusalem's new Calatrava Bridge will smell up Jerusalem, our home, for a long time to come.

Supporting the Local Economy

When Missy Older and I traveled to Israel, in 2002, on the occasion of her becoming Bat Mitzvah (family members having been lavish in their gift to her of two airline tickets), I tried to make a point of "supporting the local economy." At the time, I had figured that any money I invested in goods or services, while in the Holy Land, would help resident Jews. I was mistaken.

On the one hand, all of the eateries, where we guested, and most of the shops, where we bought presents for our generous relatives, for our other relatives, and for our friends, were Jewish-owned and staffed. Money spent at those places did fill our kin's pockets. However, in Israel, those many years ago, all was not what it appeared to be and still is often illusionary.

Consider, for example, the money I handed over to a seller of stuffed camels. Whereas it is unnecessarily to bring such kitsch, such plush beasts, back to Hutz l'Aretz, I have never been beyond engaging in such sentimental behavior. Just as I had to snap a photo of a live, four-legged Bedouin "vehicle" during that visit, I also had to have manufactured samples of the same. The problem was that I believed that by buying what I knew to be overprices goods I was helping my Israeli brothers and sisters. So, I purchased many gifts in the shop of the first hotel in which we stayed. Sadly, my acquisition of those knick-knacks did not help any Jews pay down their debts.

Other people were wise to the profit to be had from the wallets of naïve, foreign, religious Jews. Some of our ethnic cousins were running and staffing that hotel, smart in their assumption that observant Jews from distant lands might be gullible. When I learned the truth behind the character of the proprietors of the gift shop, specifically, and of the hotel management, in general, I was crushed. I was not giving over my hard earned, imported currency to helping brethren noble enough to stake a claim in the wilds of Israel. Instead, I was funding the folk who meant to drive my extended family out.

Hand wave. A decade passes. Baruch Hashem, my family makes aliyah. My husband and I merit, b'ayin tova, to watch our children grow and even to get married, here. Hopefully, we've grown, too. Heedful consumerism has become increasingly important to us. Our mindset about how to use money changed.

That shift can be marked by the adjustments that we made between the early years of our aliyah and the present. "Fryers" describes the former whereas, I hope, "fortified" describes the latter.

In our early span in Israel, a certain nonprofit organization, one to which I, as a young girl, had send my paltry coins, was revealed to honor our ethnic cousins' "right" to destroy our forests as more important than our right to improve our ecosystem. Few major news sources reported this big organization's tendency, and fewer made mention that such practices continue unabated. Simply, the fundraisers of this well-known organization look away when our relatives level prime real estate through arson, while engaging in backstage prestidigitation, the likes of which steal civil liberties from Jews who deign to protest the organization's nonsense.

When I, for instance, complained about one such, local, violation of the organization's mandate, I "got off easy" as I was merely yelled at for reporting the episode. As well, I was repeatedly hung up on, sent to voice mail, or otherwise ignored. Later, those folk tried to dissuade me from testifying to the media or the law.

Another early aliyah incident I suffered was in the marketplace. My family needed to buy appliances. We were not yet savvy to the reality that some people are so determined to be in charge of the amount and the advent of their income that they willingly step on others. In brief, my family was offered what we now refer to as "special American pricing." Based on our accents, the salespeople offered us extraordinarily inflated prices for inferior goods. Sadly, we'd assumed that folk who attend synagogue would be honest.

Then there was the family that wanted to sell us their apartment. The problem was that their unit boasted an illegal addition. Had we bought it, we would have had to pay to demolish that room. Further, a different seller wanted to charge us twice the market rate for his unit since "everyone knows" Americans come to Israel "with bags of money." What's more, when we called out those Israelis for their unscrupulous behavior, they neither denied their intentions nor apologized for trying to gyp us, but, instead, muttered something like "you won't catch me next time." I expected better behavior from kin.

These days, Computer Cowboy and I act more jaded. Last week, for example, when a cab driver tried to shoo away a second driver from making a collection, I reported the first driver. Although that first driver was from the company that I had called for my ride, he had already picked up a passenger, the lady whom the second driver was supposed to take. I refused to ride with the first driver, who was supposedly my driver, despite his protest that sharing with his extra passenger would only cause me to "detour a little" and would "save money." When I reached for my cell phone to dial his manager, he pulled away. A minute later, the other driver, the one that had been shooed, gave me the private ride I had ordered even though he wasn't my intended driver.

Also recently, on an intercity bus, some late stop, belligerent passengers decided to hold a sit in. Their choice caused us passengers who had boarded long before them to be unwillingly prevented from continuing our journey. Their sit in delayed the rest of us for a full hour. Those would-be riders thought they could make the bus company send more vehicles to their underserved stop if they held one of the company's buses hostage. While we waited for them to stop protesting, I pointed out to the ringleader that their practice was creating an ethical dilemma. Offset against any good their action might achieve was the harm they were causing the other passengers. Not surprising, that leader literally turned his back to me. Unfortunately, in the end, most of the protesters were escorted, by the police, off of the bus. No additional buses were ordered (excluding the one to the police station) *and* dozens of people were inconvenienced.

While my family's grown savvier, we've also grown more world-weary. We've seen people pose as who they're not, and we've noticed remorseless individuals cheat and steal. On balance, my family still believes that financial generosity builds schools, hospitals, mikvot, and more. Smart responses to economic quandaries, even for those of us who only dream of having "the problem" of having to wrestle with investments, remain an important part of our life.

The Cardiovascular Technologist and Others

My Israeli experiences continue to provide me, BH, with many nice surprises. Among my most recent unexpected pleasantries were my interactions with, respectively: a cardiovascular technologist, an academic department chairperson, and a utility company technician.

I encountered the cardiovascular technologist when a bit of physical distress resulted in my having to make the rounds of a few doctors. Eventually, BH, I was diagnosed with having a "Maalox moment." The docs' final assessment, however, did not come my way until after I had: electronically crossed time zones to communicate with my only sibling, engaged in "serious" talks about "the rest of life" with my two oldest children and, in general, succeeded in frightening Computer Cowboy and me quite a lot.

I don't like doctors or hospitals. In fact, I actively seek to avoid them. In spite of this fact, since the problem was in my chest, I had to follow my primary care giver's orders and bring myself to a cardiologist.

Consequently, I was alarmed. My chief doctor was suspicious of, has v'shalom, truly awful findings. There was the certainty that I would be subjected to many tests (and, if the findings were bad, also to surgery and the like). Plus, there was the reality that all of those interpositions would be *administered by doctors*!

Worse, those health care providers would speak to me in Hebrew, and, if they followed medical protocol, they would likely try to implement enough interventions to make the "cascade effect" seem like small potatoes.

Did I say I dislike doctors? I also have an allergy to drugs and to surgery. It was with no small amount of trepidation that I entered the cardiologist's office. Not only was I visiting that office with a suspected serious issue, the treatments for which are nasty, but I was also visiting an office where I would have to toss off, literally, and figuratively, any religious, personal, or other forms of modesty since, for starters, I needed an EKG/ECG.

Blessedly, Hashem pitched me a shocker; the cardiovascular technologist whom administered my exam was a woman. Issues of modesty became moot. Blessedly, that woman also spoke English, having hailed from the same country as had I. Blessedly, she was a long-time employee of that office and had even worked in cardiac care before making aliyah; there would be no Old World-style guessing on how to administer my important test. I found myself in the best of situations, during the worst of times.

The Boss was not yet done with me, however. That week, I received, BH, more unanticipated gifts. Between doctor appointments, I returned to multitasking, which, in my life includes: offering children brown rice, shooing geckos off our mirpesset, and contemplating how best to cope with my family's Nine Days' worth of piled up laundry, simultaneous with pitching ideas to a magazine editor, and poking at an incomplete essay. I was likewise: planning for Shabbat guests, and working on the menu for the forthcoming shevah brachot of one of my family's B'not Bayit. Suddenly, for the eighth or ninth time that hour, my phone rang.

My phone rings for many reasons regardless of whether I am at home, in transport, or elsewhere. When I don't answer it, I get a jangle of messages. When I do, I usually receive an ear full.

Younger Dude was calling to check whether or not I was willing to drive across the city, to pick him up if he forewent his prepaid hasa'ah. He wanted to visit a friend after camp instead of coming directly home. Missy Younger, too, had called. She wanted to know if she *really* has to complete all of her day's chores before visiting a chum in another neighborhood. Older Dude, likewise, rang up to inform me that, yet again, it was entirely my fault that his summer was being directed toward learning *Gemara* and advancing his Hebrew skills and not toward playing ball; he wanted me to know that he was holding me accountable for any day of his that was less than perfect.

Finally, Missy Older, also, called. She argued for permission: to walk to the Kotel (an hour and a half trek from our home, on a good day), to stow away at the seminary where her New World friends were learning, to visit a yeshuv in a dangerous area, to buy "sleevies," and to otherwise exercise her "maturity." Computer Cowboy, preoccupied with triaging his literally hundreds of daily international emails, did not call, except for the several times that day that he interrupted my work to make sure that I knew he still loved me.

It's of small wonder that I answer my cell phone unenthusiastically. Imagine my daze when I realized that the voice at the other end of my "electronic collar" belonged neither to any of the someones I had birthed or to that someone who helped me arrive at that state where I needed to birth. A chair of an academic unit was calling to see if I might be able to be of service to his college!

Faster than you can say "she still doesn't make kugel," I gave the man most of my divided attention. He was pleasant, the job sounded apropos for my training and experience, and, most mind-boggling of all (at least to us Old World dwellers), the salary seemed almost reasonable. I negotiated an interview date.

Thereafter, I excitedly pulled out my laptop to research the best route to his university. As quickly as my joy had blossomed, it wilted.

That institute of higher learning is located in a geographic area that is patrolled by international forces. Though I believe in my people and in our land, I also feel strongly about personal safety (remember, I don't like doctors.) I called to cancel my interview. No confirmation of my cancellation was forthcoming.

Meanwhile, I spoke to some of my Israeli girlfriends about my loss; I really had wanted to teach. One friend, alarmingly, told me stories of Israelis who had died, literally, in defending their belief that since Eretz Yisrael belonged to Am Yisrael, we should be able to have easy access to all parts of our country. Another friend, a lady fond of poking at my cultural naivety, laughed at my fear and suggested a faster, even more questionable, route from my home to the school. Fortunately, I spoke to a third pal.

That third friend reminded me that it was important for me to return to the classroom. She confided in me that she, too, was squeamish about certain of our nation's roads. Yet, my third friend reassured me that the community, in which the college is located, is a safe one to which to commute. That friend carries a gun when she drives there.

I called back the department chairman. It took only three attempts for me to reinstate my interview. Again, I received no confirmation.

The night before the originally scheduled interview date, the chair answered my electronic summons (later I found out that since he has kidlets of similar ages to mine, he ignores his cell phone - I envy his discipline.) He had never cancelled our initial meeting. Thus, he was calling to wish me well on my travels, and promised to see me in his office the following morning.

The interview was agreeable. The folk working in that department are amiable, interesting, or some combination thereof. The campus is lovely. The checkpoints on the road seem secure. Plus, I was offered the job!

I did not immediately accept it. Computer Cowboy, who is ordinarily anxious about my safety, thought I should take the offer. He pointed out, based on knowledge of me culled during our decades together, that I seem happiest when writing or teaching. The writing, BH, has been ongoing since we making aliyah, but the teaching opportunities have been spottier.

Computer Cowboy also pointed out to me that when he is "in country" he likes coming home to a happy house. He holds to the adage that "if Mom is happy, everyone is happy." He urged me to accept the job, roadways notwithstanding, and recalled to mind that I was as likely, has v'shalom, to get hurt driving in Jerusalem traffic as I was on outlying highways.

I accepted the post.

Another among that week's other unanticipated positives was the one involving a visit by our local gas company's technician. That fellow had been dispatched to our community to make appointments to check furnaces. My problem was that he was scheduling times for the same morning that close friends of ours had scheduled their youngest son's brit milah.

I explained my dilemma to the utility worker, anticipating that my poor Hebrew would only worsen the state of affairs. Much to my astonishment, upon listening to my conflict, the technician responded with a heart-warming, "no problem, I'll check your furnace today, if that's okay."

The man made good on his word. Grateful for his flexibility, I called Missy Older to help translate where necessary, and summoned Older Dude to supply the gentleman with water and small talk. Again, I experienced a wonderful turn of events.

The Soldier's Solution

Society is a fabric woven from the usual stuff. Sometimes, it's accented with sparkly bits indigenous to a particular segment of its population. In other words, it is simultaneously true that people tend to behave the same no matter where you drop them and that human behavior is influenced by environment. Take the case of the IDF soldiers who were snacking at a local mall.

I merited witnessing those soldiers' goings-on because I was dutifully "resting" between an acupuncture appointment and my date with an elliptical training machine. My care providers have been insisting that I pause between interventions. I translated that prescription as necessitating my eating a salad whose leaves someone else had checked for bugs and whose peppers someone else had diced.

Given my middle-aged mindfulness, I scanned the food court for an almost clean spot. In the back of the hall, I saw a table empty of people and underpopulated by debris. Best yet, that seat was adjacent to a table filled with soldiers.

Granted, those members of the military might be all that stands between my family's safety and a bad outcome, has v'shalom, during a crisis, yet, I cannot help but experience members of the armed forces as someone else's adorable, albeit responsible, children. The fellows, who were occupying the table next to mine, looked to be somewhere between eighteen and twenty, an age for which I have an affinity. As a professor, I regularly interact with that age group. As a mom of older teens, I constantly have that stage of life floating around my salon or sticking its head in my refrigerator. Hence, for me, being able to sit near those dear boys meant getting a good vibe to go along with my salad.

Initially, those young gentlemen were all macho business. I sucked in my cheeks so they wouldn't see me smiling. My own children have lectured me that visible fondness is off-putting. So, instead, I listened attentively to their talk and stole as many glances in their direction as seemed reasonable for a person of my demographics. Fortunately, the boys didn't notice me eavesdropping.

Rather, they barked in Hebrew, in Russian, and in English into their cell phones, growled, in a friendly manner at each other, and did whatever else it took to set their world right. Shortly after they established their temporal-spatial parameters, two of the trio left their table. I assumed they were going to order food and were leaving the last one behind as a lookout. I was wrong.

I paid more attention to my greens. Too quickly, I got to the bottom of my bowl. Fortunately, the youngsters returned before I ate my last sliver of tomato. They did not come back with trays of hot food. Rather, they brought with them a filled paper bag!

I let my eyes wander once more to their side of the divide. Experience dictates that boys that age will eat almost anything. I wondered what was so precious that they brought it into the food court. My curiosity was soon sated.

From within the depths of their sack, one of the soldiers removed three little, plastic spoons and a large carton of ice cream. In short notice, those three boys were cooing like small brothers who had found their mom's cookie stash. Their tough posturing melted faster than the sweet treat set before them.

When I finished my blessings and got up to leave, I looked again at those valiants. Once more, I smiled. Those guardians of our nation were still speaking to each other in soft voices and were still enjoying their "illicit" snack.

Another Dumpster Fire

More than a decade ago, after my family had made aliyah, I was radicalized by the thought that folk, here, voice their disapproval of public policy by destroying public property. I have seen many instances of the handiwork of such dissent. Mostly, I have witnessed the destruction of dumpsters, but I have also observed social unrest in the form of graffitied signs and broken street lights. That these events are tied to collective displeasure is clear from mediated statements made by the responsible groups.

I don't like paying taxes to clean up, to replace, or to otherwise compensate for my cohorts' restlessness. I don't like feeling as though I can't walk on certain street because I fear that the same others who break fixtures might break noggins. I'm not proud to be part of any group that promotes such actions. On balance, my kin are not cowardly or reticent.

At any rate, the flames that keep the local dumpster cats at bay, in the middle of the night, in the parking lot nearest my family's apartment, might not issue from the instigation of any social movement's leader. I live in a quiet community, far away, b'ayin tova, from targets that seem newsworthy; it takes me a long bus ride to get to the center of town.

More likely, someone tossed a cigarette stub into the filled trash receptacle. Such mindlessness, however, is not necessarily less problematic than is the intentional ruin of shared material goods. An unwillingness to be accountable for (un)intentional vandalism disturbs me more than does directed destruction; material-based protests, though unconscionable, are logical.

Whereas I don't believe any humans were harmed (mercifully, during the night in question, the parking lot, where the dumpster sits, was not packed, as it ordinarily is, with cars. In fact, for reasons literally only known in Heaven, the spaces to either side of the dumpster were empty) and whereas I think that the currently pregnant dumpster cats that frequent that bin might be able to find food elsewhere, much harm, nonetheless, was done. Someone living in or visiting my community destroyed a dumpster and endangered man and beast because of his or her lack of culpability.

This event drew only one police car, but no "curious neighbors" swarmed to nose out or to otherwise witness the goings on. As long as folk are, accordingly, not made to be unanswerable for their deeds, they will continue to fall away from socially-sanctioned behavior toward dangerous instances of social roughness. The more wild members we have in our collective, the more problems we have.

Consider, another, related case. Every year, before Passover, neighborhood folk burn their chametz on the hillside, beyond the fence, past the dumpster. Unfortunately, those same individuals, after igniting their piles, literally turn their backs on their flaming crusts and walk away. Every year, it follows that grasses and other forbs go up in smoke. Cats, birds, and hedgehogs get displaced. Homes get subjected to fumes. Children, who frequently are inadequately minded, risk stepping on coals and playing with flames.

To boot, one year, a majestic pine tree, the former crown of this area's hill, caught fire and died. That tree, though, took about two years to fall, meanwhile endangering all of the children that play, and all of the critters that live, on that little swath of land. There's more. Less important, but certainly annoying, last week, someone, judging from the size of the discards, with a medium-sized dog, allowed their pup to empty itself all along the sidewalk in front of my apartment building and in front of an adjoining one. At least this messy event was not life-threatening.

It's both dangerous and inconvenient to live among others who are so inwardly focused (in an egocentric, not in a G-d-centric, spiritual fashion) as to act out all of their unresolved toddler developmental processes on public holdings. Disagreeable behaviors issuing from others' planned or accidental heedlessness are wrong and stupid. At least rioters attach meaning to what they are doing.

We live in the holiest place. We ought to be more mindful about our deeds.

The Challot and the Kallot

After three weary nights of trying to help with shidduchim, I opted for a morning off. Rather than bid my family adieu for the day and hide in the sanctuary that is my office, I asked Computer Cowboy if he minded my taking his place in driving the kids to school. My man was good with the plan as he was overworked; he nearly flew to the first bus which would return him to his source code. For my part, I marshaled the gathering of lunches, of books, of children, and of shoes.

By the time that the children and I left, we were only ten minutes off schedule. I deposited only one of them at the wrong corner (Missy Older got to walk a few extra blocks.) Unfortunately, my head was still whirling with thoughts about the matches I had tried to aid the night before.

I am not a professional shadchan. I am not a rabbi, a therapist, or a lawyer. I am a people person. I am trained to teach human communication and to express myself about a few related topics. Nonetheless, both here, in The Old World, and there, in The New World, I was approached by friends to join circles of women who try to help other Jews find spouses.

Whereas, during our post-college days, Computer Cowboy and I danced at the weddings of friends I had matched up, we have danced at far fewer of those events in our middle years. In fairness, as undergraduates, we were young and the brides and grooms I connected were young. Today, the brides and grooms I try to unite range, typically, from their thirties to their sixties.

Nevertheless, as compensation for the emotional gymnastics I just performed in the name of the mitzvah of shidduchim (most seekers of mates need reassurance, reframing, and above all, a listening ear), I planned to drive to a special, distant bakery for my family's weekly challah; I find it nurturing to ride around with open windows in the sweet Jerusalem sunshine.

When I arrived at the bakery, the mini pitas, which my children adore, the wheat-free cookies, which my children need, and the too-good-not-to-buy-at-least-one parve cakes, over which my children would later argue, were ready. Yet, the challot were still baking.

Since I had already indulged myself with my ride to the bakery, and since I had other tasks I could complete in that part of town, I paid for my selections, promised to return in an hour and went on my way. We don't always get what we want when we want it. Sometimes, we get something better. Always, we have to wait for Hashem's sanction.

Analogously, one of the people I was trying to set up was rather receptive to all sorts of demographic possibilities…that is, until I called her back to talk to her about a man I had formerly interviewed. Suddenly, this woman set limits on categories about which she had expressed openness just a day earlier.

In the same way, there was a fellow, whom I was trying to put together with a lady, whose stats matched his stats nicely. It didn't hurt my presentation of her case that while I quizzed that lady, I developed a fondness for her. Unfortunately, the fellow's contact person turned out to be his protective mother. Suffice it to say that several phone calls later, it was the mother, not the perspective groom, who called to explain that there would be no initial date.

Such happenstances are, unfortunately, typical in the realm of shidduchim. I remember, from my time in the States, a young man with whom I was trying to work. Hashem put a possible bride for him into my head and Hashem made their first date successful.

Nevertheless, the young man refused to consider a second date with that possible bride. After much wheedling on my part, the young man admitted that the young lady was "not pretty enough" for him. To no avail, I attempted to broaden his perspective (i.e. what was *he* going to look like in five or ten years.) So, I told him off, and dropped him from my roster. Months later, I ran into him and his new wife. Objectively speaking, the woman whom the young man had rejected was far more attractive than the one he had married. Go figure.

Before you say I am crass and otherwise without any concept of the pain involved in seeking a mate, consider the following. My husband and my children have witnessed the hours of tears I've cried here, and in The New World, over shidduchim. Moreso, they have witnessed the hours of prayers I've spoken here, and in The New World, on behalf of the people I try to help. Whereas my matchmaking is totally private, my reactions to my efforts are often played out in the public space of my family's salon since I like hugs when I feel discouraged.

Sure, I've been called on to smooth away the prewedding jitters of folk of both genders. Sure, my husband and I have had the bracha to attend weddings of never-before-married people in their forties or fifties. Sure, my entire family has aided me in making sheva brachot for some of the people I've merited to help. Sure, we've been invited to subsequent Brit Milot. Baruch Hashem for those facts!

Still, in spite of the sma'achot, which my family and I have been honored to attend because of my matchmaking work, such celebrations do nothing to alleviate the anguish I feel over every person who remains unattached. Their shattered dreams are my pain.

I'm not fooling myself; The Boss, not any human agency, determines couples. In view of that, I cry and I pray.

At the most recent of shidduch circles, we women discussed involving our husbands and our rabbanim in our efforts. We need their input not so much for questions of Halacha (it's a given that we seek Torah sources for direction), but for the purpose of broadening our access to unmarrieds. The couplehood crisis affects Jews of all stripes, of all ages and of both genders. We need the reliable men in our lives to help us connect to more people.

I think the solution to the problem of lonely Jews can be found in the achdut of Klal Yisrael. More specifically, the person who didn't work out for your date might be perfect for your roommate, for your brother, for your learning partner, or for your subordinate. The clerk in the grocery store needs a husband as much as does the president of the bank. At the end of the day, people crave companionship. People want committed relationships.

So, if you are sought by a single that needs to unburden, listen! You do not have to fix anything; you just need to listen. You can provide a great service simply by beholding another person's circumstances. More broadly, as a community, we are quick to network for jobs and for other manners of money, but somewhat slow to network for marriages and for other significant social matters.

I completed my errands in that faraway part of Jerusalem, even finding the time to purchase the imported ketchup adored by Missy Younger. I returned to the bakery. Not only were my challot just coming out of the oven (the car smelled sooo good on route home), but almost every member of the bakery staff warmly greeted me when I returned.

True, I had had to wait and I had had to decide whether or not I was willing to change my schedule. Those steps were my histadlut. Similarly, it is the case that folk in the shidduch parsha have to take all of the necessary steps.

I felt better about my choice when the bakery staff cheered my return. Let's help singles feel better about their efforts by encouraging them to continue their efforts.

The Path of Torah *is* the Path of the Feminist

When it comes to gender roles, we need to ask ourselves whether or not we should allow ourselves to be mired in the divisiveness of hierarchies fulled by gender biased assumptions about social positions' relative worth. Neutralizing the dissonance that is created by viewing tradionional women's roles as being valuable only when those positions are esteemed as comparable to contemporarily-defined or androcentrically-defind statues is of limited use. Also limited is embodiment of that dissonance.

More specifically, defining our personal importance (if we are female) or the worth of women, in general (whether we are female or not), entirely, or even partially, by behaviors that are socially, especially androcentrically, measured (explicitly, by earned degrees, by titles, by publications, and by the like) is dubious. We need to get beyond that practice.

More exactly, its useful to determine whether or not any part of our internal conflict associated with evaluating contemporarily-defined women's roles, is based on a belief that traditional women's roles are less valuable than are traditional men's roles or than contemporarily-defined women's roles. It's of great utility, too, to figure out why we are uncomfortable engaging in discourse about, or privately contemplating, the merit of traditional women's roles. We need to ask ourselves how our ideals (i.e. those ideas which we are most likely to hold as true) differ from our behaviors (i.e. those acts which we are most likely to perform) for each of these points. When we find disparity, we are making progress.

If we fail to find discrepancy, we need to delve further - ideological incommensurability is only as overpowering as are our unchallenged personal prejudices. Our society can be enhanced if we are careful in observing: the quality of our inner lives; the service, rather than the self-gratification, yielded by our relationships; and the quality of our connection with our Creator. It is advantageous for us: to go beyond androcentrically-produced norms for personal worth, to mistrust norms predisposed against female-generated epistemologies, and to cultivate comfort with discourse and contemplation that concern themselves with behaviors associated with traditional women's roles.

To support notions about the Feminist Paradigm, we can continue to look toward the words of individuals who are recognized within academia, and who, hence, continue to use credentialing to buffer their arguments. Nevertheless, to support notions about Torah Judaism, we *must* take the writings generated by the Creator as primary, and the writings provided by historically esteemed Rabbis as secondary (writings produced by lesser lights, such as academic scholars, it follows, have less worth.)

Accordingly, "Torah Judaism" is that *topos,* which simultaneously *prescribes* life as governed by living the mandates of the Torah and as governed by studying the Torah's mandates, whereas "the Feminist Paradigm" is a series of fluctuating *topoi,* which refer to life as a series of *described* behaviors governed by conflicting individual and societal needs/wants.

We should care that Torah Judaism and that the Feminist Paradigm differ in their state of fixedness because, as Jews, we are accountable for freeing ourselves from the pervading power of "manufactured ideologies" produced by specialists. As Jews, we also have a religiously-induced role in creating collective peace.

Providentially, we are equipped with tools to meet those goals. We can draw out our society's rhetorical fiends by deconstructing seemingly polarized systems' rhetorical acts and by translating those deconstructed acts into fresh interpretations of social reality. Note, our understanding, not our behaviors, is what consequently changes.

For instance, my commitment to my Torah lifestyle is not an undesirable role of social enslavement, i.e. a sign of my being a deficient person, but is *the desirable* role of the socially *empowered,* i.e. a sign of my being a complete person. Moreso, my role as a Torah Jew augments any previously sanctioned roles, e.g. any academic training/credentialing, which I have, since my Torah role is what legitimizes me and grants me my rights.

In so much as I am glad that I home birthed my babies, nursed them, and boosted their health with herbal tinctures created by my own hands, I am at least equally as glad that I worked and continue to work to uphold the articles of faith of my people. The role of Jewish women is subtle. Our role is to open portals to forbearance, to understanding, and to unity, and to lend a hand to other persons whom seek the same. The laws of the Torah do not challenge feminism, but enhance it.

As a community, we are obliged to go beyond androcentrically-produced norms for personal worth, specifically, and to mistrust norms predisposed against female-generated epistemologies, in general. We must cultivate comfort with discourse and contemplation that concern themselves with behaviors associated with traditional women's roles. We need to strive to overcome the forces that use social paradoxes to continue to invalidate women; we need to utilize authority that overarches the status quo, to incorporate an acknowledgment of the legitimacy of the Creator's Word into our days and nights.

When we, as a society, authentically accept, at the highest levels of abstraction, the possibility of the correctness of women's roles as differing from those of men, we will repair ourselves. Such reparations are invaluable.

Visiting the Kotel

In the heart of the Old City, in this world's epicenter, a fundamental tradition of our forefathers continues. There, at the Western Wall, The Wailing Wall, The Kotel, the last remaining portion of our Temple, the site of our future Beit HaMikdash, we Jews gather.

At this holy site, we assemble to pray for health, for prosperity, for happiness, and for Moshiach. Our words of longing fly heavenward in Hebrew, in English, in Russian, in European languages, in Amharic, and in the entirety of the tongues of the seventy nations.

At this singular place, our hands, young and otherwise, stretch to clasp the holiness, to beg for mercy, to exclaim Providence. Under this wall's shy boughs of caper flowers, we extend ourselves to strengthen the triple cords of generations former, future, and present.

There, we unite our psyches with the fabric of the cosmos, amplify our gratitudes and increase the energy of our requests. At The Kotel, amidst pleas stuffed into that not-so-simple edifice's crevices, we palpate our hearts and sing directly to The Boss. We connect to HaKodesh Baruchu and shimmer brightly in response to His Presence.

Some of us supplicants appear in jeans and T-shirts, others of us arrive in traditional dress. Whereas our clothing, like our lived days and nights, reduces us to traditions upheld or lost, such artifacts do not hamper our praying. There might be separate sections for men and for women, but there is no exclusion at The Wall.

Our neshemot, no matter the fabric or the deeds in which they come dressed, know this singular location to be a very powerful conduit to the Almighty. Our neshemot, no matter how tutored in Torah or not, feel the energy at this juncture, feel, how at this place, time and space are suspended.

Against those impossibly large stone squares, our heritage streams, and our spiritual mailboxes open. In that spot, unlike any other, we are released from mundanities as we fasten to the sacred. There, friction among our tribes, and between us and other nations, is suspended. Impediments between our knowledge and True Knowing are lifted. Blocks, which might otherwise distance us from our Maker, become as nothing.

Albeit, sma'achot, such as Bnai Mitzvot, weddings, IDF initiations, and other important life cycle events utilize The Western Wall as their anchor. True, "dignitaries," from media stars to political icons, use the Wailing Wall as a means of validation. Nonetheless, it is the simple visits of simple people, of the dust that constitutes rocks and of the rocks that build our Temple, which give continual and layered significance to our journeys and meaning to our service.

May each of us merit visiting Israel, walking in Jerusalem, and praying at The Kotel, soon. May Moshiach make himself known. Amen. – Hannah

****

A three year-old, for whom I used to babysit for, once explained to me that we don't eat on Tish B'Av because the "Big Hamantaschen" was destroyed. For her, the loss of an oversized cookie was reason enough to fast.

Even though I know a bit more about the Beit HaMikdash and about the chorban than she did, it used to be hard for me to relate to Tish B'Av's fast. It was hard for me to miss something, The Temple, which I never had.

II have yet to have the zehut to eat a Chorbon Pesach or to hear the Temple's Kohanim sing. My Chorbon Pesach is the shank bone on my family's Seder plate and my songs are the "Shir Shel Yom" that I sing, every day, at the end of my tefillot. I know that something is missing, but, before experiencing it, I struggled to feel the loss.

When I got to The Kotel, when I saw the remaining wall from our Holy Temple, I started to understand what I am missing.
It's not so much seeing the wall, itself, as seeing the activity taking place

there that helped me understand the loss. When at The Kotel, I felt closer to my nation than when I stood in any other place. When at The Kotel, I felt connected to that slice of time when Am Yisrael was not split by prejudices. When at The Kotel, I saw true Ahavat Yisrael.

Today, I can sit for hours, there, and just watch the spectrum of our people that visit, and just listen to the multitude of their languages. The Kotel's visitors wear lots of different fashions and come from many different backgrounds. Today, praying at The Kotel inspires me.

Over there, stand Charaedi women, in long black skirts, rocking double strollers, while swaying back and forth in earnest prayer. Not far from them are members of a French tour group, who wear borrowed scarves tied over their trendy jeans and who pose for pictures in front of The Wall. To their side are American seminary students, decked out in their graduating class sweatshirts, and praying from their trusty Art Scroll siddurim.

All of those people are different, but all of them are the same. On the outside, there is nothing that connects them. There are teachers, housewives, and business women. On the inside, though, all of them are Jews, connected by The Kotel, by their roots.

With Moshiach coming any day, we must now, more than ever, work on seeing ourselves in every Jew. It might be hard to recognize ourselves in persons appearing different from us, but we must try. We're pretty much alike beneath the surface.

Take a minute to appreciate others as part of the whole, instead of regarding them as representing ways of dressing or as representing levels of accomplishment. In seeing Jews as a people, we become prepared to greet Moshiach. May he come quickly! - Rivka

Worldly Reactions to Israel

Why the Sudden Interest

Europeans and North Americans are getting antsy. The uprisings taking place in Libya, in Tunisia, in Yemen, in Iran, in Iraq, in Bahrain, in Egypt, and in Algeria, are making residents of the quartet nations uneasy.

It's not enough, for example, that Malmö, Sweden is garnering more of a reputation for violence than for shipbuilding or for medical research, and that a British Muslim cleric recently called on the President of the United States to either embrace Islam or to face punishment under Sharia Law. Moreso, it seems to be the case that the oil barons, once more, are wagging other nations' access to the greater part of global oil reserves under those nations' chins. Note: stories about Middle Eastern and African rebellions are often placed in written venues, or spoken in oral ones, alongside of stories about increasing gas prices. Accordingly, regular folk, people accustomed to comfortable living, have become afraid; they don't want their life styles altered.

So, the phone calls have begun. Not looking to improve relationships with, or to aid, Israelis, but seeking, from Israelis, phantasms of reassurance, ordinary people, ones who would usually disassociate themselves from the goings-on of "remote" regions of the world, are acting on their worries. No longer is it enough for those persons to be media jocks seated in front of television or computer screens, half attending to world news, especially to news of foreigners' difficulties, before returning their minds to contemplating the next grocery shop, the next business transaction, or the next PTO meeting. Those legions now want to impact the events of our state, or to solicit from us the guarantee that they don't have to worry.

Correspondingly, those individuals are increasingly contacting their friends and family, even their nominal associates, in the Holy Land, to demand answers. Those others, for the most part, want us locals to prophesize that all will once more be well, here. As was true before, is true at present; we Israelis watch and respond to the Arabs, to the Persians, and to the Africans in the same fashion as does everyone else; it's just that unrest in this locality is troubling to the world's bystanders.

Whereas this land is sacred to Hashem, Israelis are still obliged to do our histadlut. Although nearly all of our boys and many of our girls sacrifice their prime, and, sometimes, their lives, to serve in the IDF, we are only humanly empowered to impact our neighbors. Perhaps, we are less empowered to make a difference than are the mighty nations situated offshore.

Nonetheless, others implore us to do something, anything. Those outlanders demand to hear fabricated words about safety, i.e. about increased stability in the Middle East, and about Israel's ability to provide protection both for its citizens and for its allies.

We promise nothing of that sort. While Israel wants to be powerful, only The Boss controls outcomes. We can, and maybe ought, however, to ask why Western Civilization suddenly needs to know that we Israelis are fine, that we Israelis will make the world safer than it might actually be, and that any strengths we Israelis have will continue to be manifested.

Consider that a lot of those others were on vacation, literally, and figuratively, during the Second Lebanon War of 2006, missing not only the conflict but also that the IDF experienced many casualties. They neglected to attend to the fact that Al Jazeera reported on the details of the war, i.e. publicized the locations of Israeli fighters.

Similarly, few of our foreign acquaintances protested Israelis having to yield her sovereign territory in 2005, or protest, at present, their leaders pressuring us to *not build homes* for our people. Apparently, such concerns don't tie into their need for good gas prices.

Likewise, during the Gulf War of 1991, the conflict during which Israel was bid to sit on its hands while being bombarded, many of those residents of democratic nations, of societies based on Biblical teachings, muttered pity and compassion out one side of their mouths, while articulating relief, at not having to deal with the Islamic scourge, out the other. Today, too, those other nations, if silenced with lullabies from our lips, are happy to return to complacent head games, in which Israelis are alternatively, and arbitrarily, rubricked as "good" or "bad." and in which those outsiders take little or no culpability for Middle Eastern incidents.

In 1982, as another case in point, during the First Lebanon War: Operation Peace for Galilee, Israeli settlers had to defend their homes, their lands, and their existence, against Syrian terrorists. Then, as now, armchair warriors, located elsewhere on the globe, either screamed for peace at the cost of Israeli lives or ignored the conflagration altogether. The Falklands War, Prince Williams' birth, and the faltering ERA seemed to make for more acceptable foci than did the possible loss of a significant chunk of Israel.

Whereas many Jews of Diaspora and their friends felt pride at the outcome of the Yom Kippur Way of 1973 and at the results of the Six Day War of 1967, few did more than don blue and white clothing or search for recipes for pita and falafel when those conflicts ended. Equally, the 1968 War of Attrition received less needed rhetorical or actual support than did the peace talks which followed. Historically, outside "thinkers" have launched anti-Israel diatribes from points around the world when not altogether ignoring matters of Israel's security.

As per the Sinai Campaign of 1956 and the 1947 War of Independence, the record shows that apathy, not support, dominated most lands' stance toward the nascent, modern State of Israel. With friends like that, we added to our enemies.

Today, simultaneous with us Israelis saluting the valent deeds of our former heroes, both hidden and known, and with us praying that current happenstances don't cause us to need more patriots, the world, or at least powerful portions of it, turns to us for succor. It's confounding that other nations have the audacity to force us to abandon our homes and our lives, yet insist that we reassure them that we are still playing on their team or, that our team will yet fight the good fight, even if such a scenario means we have to succeed in battle without their support.

It follows, therefore, that it's not surprising that when Europeans and North Americans call us, not as government representatives, not as businessmen, but as plain folk in quest of comfort, we take umbrage. We Israelis have better things to do, like making sure that our kids survive to see the next morning, like reinforcing our national defense system, like praying past the point at which we thought we could pray no more, than holding those others' hands.

Truly Alone

During March, 2011, the Shacharit prayers of a handful of Mexican Jews, who were traveling on an Alaska Airlines jet, caused those Jews to be arrested upon deboarding.[17] Apparently, those men's tefillin spooked some of the flight crew.

A little more than a year ago, a similar incident occurred on a US Airways flight.[18] Likewise, a tefillin-wearing Yid caused a panic on a New Zealand boat last year,[19] and another Yid,[20] one praying on a Chicago train, a few years prior, too, caused a bit of mayhem.

Those events, sadly, typify the totality of the nations' ongoing ignorance and their lack of concern about that ignorance of Yiddishkeit. Such unwarranted apathy is not surprising; historically, we Jews have been regularly cast off by other people. There's something substantial to the notion, broadcast in the 33rd section of *Tehillim,* that we ought not to trust <u>in political lead</u>ers or in their engines of power, but only in The Almighty.

17. Reuters. "Jews Wearing Tefillin Cause Alarm Aboard Airplane." *The Jerusalem Post.* 13. Mar., 2011. http://www.jpost.com/Jewish-World/Jewish-News/Jews-wearing-tefill-incause-alarm-aboard-airplane.

18. David Warner and Larry McShane. "Jewish teen's tefillin sets off bomb scare that diverts US Airways flight from LaGuardia Airport [sic]." *Daily News.* 21 Jan., 2010. http://www.nydailynews.com/news/national/jewish-teen-tefillin-sets-bomb-scare-diverts-airways-flight-laguardia-airport-article-1.183107.

19. Jonathan Kalmus. "The 'tefillin terrorist' and a New Zealand ferry [sic]." *The Jewish Chronicle.* 13 Dec., 2010. https://www.thejc.com/news/world/the-tefillin-terrorist-anda-scare-on-a-new-zealand-ferry-1.20008.

20. Itamar Eichner. "Is that a bomb strapped to your head? [sic]" *YNet.* 11 Nov., 2007. https://www.ynetnews.com/articles/0%2C7340%2CL-3477136%2C00.html.

Consistently, only Hashem has partnered with us.

More than two millennia ago, in Shushan, we stood by ourselves, facing the enmity of all of the kingdoms of the Persian Empire (hence, Purim). Nearly one thousand years ago, we were expelled from England, from Spain, and from Portugal. Two hundred years ago, we suffered from pogroms in Russia. A generation ago, the Shoah occurred with the world watching, but doing nothing, as millions of us were massacred in multiple lands. In the time of Moshiach, it is said, we will again stand by ourselves, that is, without human aid. Today, during the chronological bridge between ancient and future spans, we remain truly alone, as well.

Whereas the Alaska Airlines officials' inanity, insensitivity, lack of appropriate knowledge, wrongful use of power, etc., are offensive, unethical, even illegal, the more frightening aspect of this story is the response of the masses to the representation of the affair. Specifically, several thousand readers added their thoughts to the comments section of that article.[21] Most of those writers were openly hostile to Jews.

Consider, that in light of forthcoming elections in the United States, in light of the unspeakable combined disasters of earthquake, tsunami, and radioactive releases in Japan, in light of the fizzling rebellion in Libya, in light of the notorious Broadway musical that has yet to enjoy an official opening night, or in light of the many other existent "widely appealing" new topics referring to world leaders, to economic downturns, or to schemes for getting rich, those commenters had bothered both to read that short article and to respond to it with malign language.

Most of those persons were unapologetically anti-Semitic in their remarks, lumping Jews and Muslims together, in general, and devout Jews and suicidal Muslims together, more exactingly. Those respondents also invited Jews and Muslims to resolve their differences via mutual genocide, and called for democracies to ban together to eliminate Jews. Albeit, some of those people "merely" decried organized religion, per se, or Judaism, more principally or "simply" sprinkled their words with

---

21. I'm referring to readers' response to a Yahoo News version of that news. Sadly, neither the original Yahoo article nor an archived version of it is available any longer.

crude language or with name calling of a sinister nature. Other readers, on balance, scapegoated Jews for the TSA's inconvenient, preposterous, even draconian security measures and for the many acts of terrorism for which our foes not only claimed responsibility, but for which government agencies independently tagged those horrors. In other words, in that article's comments section, Jews were stigmatized, marginalized, delegitimized, and overall demonized.

Granted, there is very little censorship of readers' responses to web articles. Granted, few policy makers attend to the sentiments expressed by folk flexing their keyboard polemics. Granted, sticks, stones, intercontinental ballistic missiles, and salted (nuclear) bombs can be more devastating than words. However, the implicitly approved discourse found in such widely-attended rant sessions, too, can create incalculable damage.

Those persons, the ones who elected to respond to that fairly unimportant news piece, are the same people who fight in militaries, who do triage in hospitals, who vote for government officers, who urge their leaders not to support Israel, and who encourage the world, via Blackberry, IMing, Tweeting, and others modes of convergent media, to ignore, or, worse, to demonize, Jewish suffering. In particular, that same day when thousands of free citizens were razing Jews over our legitimate expression of religion, few write-ups were found on the web, or elsewhere, save for pro-Israel sites, such as *Arutz Sheva*, about the massacre of the Jewish family from Yeshuv Itamar. In fact, Israeli police have been aiding the world's habit of relegating Jews to insignificant social standing by trying to enforce a news blackout on the Itamar murders.

All in all, we Jews cannot and ought not to rely on the possibility of friendship from other nations. We should not believe that noncritical thinking types of folk will suddenly be rational about world events and we would be foolish to believe that human mouthpieces, the ones that are able to make rational arguments, will necessarily slant their discourse in our favor. As before and as will be in times to come, we are Hashem's people, but among the nations, we Jews stand without help.

Unbelievable

In the past, I've addressed the issue of folk, who present the news in a direct way, while trying to literally profit from other peoples' losses, and the issue of folk, who act as though they could not care less about their neighbors' plights, ignoring or even causing those difficulties. Now, I'm turning my attention to folk, who twist the facts in order to buffet their sense of personal worth, and to irresponsible government officials.

I'm a middle-aged mom trying to live a life centered on spiritual principals. Hence, I am less than wowed when allegedly well-intended "friends" excitedly contact me to "congratulate" me on our Holy Land's most recent "investment in peace." Spinning works for music at nightclubs, not for the words and deeds of patriots.

I'm no follower of the discothèque scene, no urban girl waiting to get beyond velvet ropes, no wannabe hoping to be singled out for admission to some selective social brouhaha. I don't serve myself up as one more supplicant to other peoples' opinions on, or off, any dance floor. To wit, I'm not at all excited about trading my brother and sister's blood, specifically, or their safety, in general, for international kowtowing. I get no excitement from: giving up our collective peace of mind, from backing down in the South, from pulling back at the Lebanon border, or from withdrawing anywhere in our dear land, in exchange for some variety of amorphic, "altruistic" rewards splashed, only for a mere day or so, across the headlines of venues like *The New York Times* or *Yahoo News.*

Consequently, my response to my less-than-mindful, apparently resource-poor (they lack enough time, money or energy to ask a few questions, to do a bit of research, or to think critical about global situations) friends is anything from a blasé "I'm not in favor of the most recent international resolution to our ongoing conflict" to a strident "are you kidding me? Such a decree is poison to Israel's wellbeing. Surely you mean to say/write that you want me and my dear ones to be out of harm's way."

Superstorm Sandy aside, too many folk, who are living in Hutz L'Aretz, sleep better when wearing their eye masks and ear plugs than they do when allowing themselves to be exposed to actual goings-on. It's too bad that feigning to "see no evil and to hear no evil" produces nothing more utilitarian than denial. Woe to contemporary civilization if the day comes when our alleged gatekeepers of freedom, the media, stop selectively reporting, or when our politically well-muscled counterparts stop feeding the masses ideas that leave citizens cognitively unchallenged.

Note that there were disproportionately few, if any, descriptions, even in blogs, tweets, and others of the available, relatively individualized, means of getting the word out, of the bravery performed by, of the lives lost by, or of limbs risked by Israelis who made insane efforts to insure our enemy's well-being. Instead, news outlets elected to send dramatic footage of carnage on the other side of the fence. As well, those sources seemed to experience no umbrage when reframing, editing, or otherwise disfiguring, reality. It's not just movie directors who work to make fantasy seem like verity.

In fact, some of those doctored dramatizations were so unreal as to have taken place in lands geographically removed from the battle in Gaza. Others were completely staged. Consider the Syrian infighting identified incorrectly as civilian losses caused by Israel's army. Consider the "bloodied casualties" that got up from their prone positions when they thought the cameras had stopped rolling.

If overt distortions of truth are insufficient, we can entertain ourselves with other distractions. Why seek social accountability when we can stay focused on Thanksgiving, on December holidays, on newly released movies, on fashion finds, etc.? This season, La La Land is for sale for only a fraction of one's soul.

That infamous international coterie, that group of politicos that make nations and would-be states retract announcements of cease fires until their delegates arrive for photo ops, and those formerly self-described hawkish local chiefs, the ones who lived for decades among select sentiments only to cave under world pressure, teach us that Jewish blood is insignificant, and that Israel is akin to the smart child in the idiots' classroom, who gets shushed, repeatedly, so that the other kids won't look so bad. Simply, Israel ceased and desisted to defend herself, despite her strategic advantage, because bullies said she had to.

Whereas many pundits have argued that money turned those negotiations, that the more dominant countries had thrown fiduciary bones to their military pets, I'm not convinced that international relations are so simple. A people that turns swamps into metropolises, that teaches the world how to farm in wastelands, and that implements surgical strikes, i.e. that successfully minimalizes the collateral damage of an opponent that has proven its lack of qualms about using children, even infants, as human shields, or about hiding armaments in places of worship, in schools, or in hospitals, that is, in locations ordinarily considered too sacrosanct to be involved in matters of war, is not going to be readily swayed by the dollar, the euro, or the yen. The fellows that steer this nation are not insipient. A different sort of malodor wafts from their traitorous behavior.

Less than two weeks after the first sirens sounded in Jerusalem, officials tried to turn our attention to other things. It might seem convenient to walk away from Pillar of Cloud, but it's not prudent. We are doomed to repeat experiences for which we've failed to tether discourse to reality, to grasp integral truths, or to invite accuracy home. We pause, but the enemy reloads. From our leaders, we receive no answerability.

Our "friends," both individuals and nations, privately, as well as via the media, are negligent in wanting us to shrug and to act as if all is well. It's of no small wonder that life in these parts remains unbelievable.

Idolatry and the Mass Media

I used to think that we are more sensible than dumb brutes, such as cows. Cows feel no compulsion to emulate each other. They might be territorial, they might be smelly, and they might even be "moo-dy" when mating or protecting their young, yet cows are able to accept their given roles.

Not so, us silly humans. Certainly, we are territorial (never try to move a little Jewish grandmother from a bus seat. Not only is such a behavior unconscionable, but it is also dangerous.) Certainly, we are smelly (all of that charif we eat exudes from our pores.) Certainly, we are moody (husbands ought to come equipped with sensors that inform them exactly what their wives need to hear, even if their wives, ever so "innocently," set up communication paradoxes.) Certainly, we strive to protect our young (Israeli parents are infamous for the stands they take with their children's relatives, friends, and teachers. Israeli parents are equally infamous for forgetting that those relatives, friends, and teachers likewise use Israeli conversational norms.) Humans, however, seem ill content to stick to their given roles.

Academics and other social gatekeepers have long lamented the mass media's contribution to this breakdown of individual integrity. The media's speed, their broad distribution, and their ability to screen messages all have been lambasted by our social sentries. Our protectors, similarly, have proclaimed that if the mass media were a bit pokier, e.g. only able to convey messages at the velocity of a politician elocuting at a public ceremony, the mass media might be less influential.

Our protectors, similarly, have proclaimed that if the mass media were a bit more stymied in their dissemination of ideas, e.g. were only able to effect the populous at the rate of a third grader participating in a Chanukah play, the mass media might be less influential. Our protectors have also claimed that if the mass media were unedited, e.g. if they were as polished as a New World uncle giving over his thoughts at a Shabbat table, on the halacha of challah knives, the mass media might be less influential.

Yet, despite the cry of our "moral vanguards" (it's nice to engage in admonishments from time to time to disprove the veracity of Jews being stereotyped as unusually skilled in this form of rhetoric), our contemporary mass media are fast, are well circulated, and are very, very enhanced. Pointing fingers at them does not lead to a win.

Although many religious homes eschew certain electronic media such as movies and television, and, to a lesser extent, the Internet, these same homes, often, allow radio, books, and periodicals. Furthermore, even if all texts, electronic or otherwise, which enter a home, are censored for content and language, it is still possible for the Yetzer Hara to slip in.

The arrangement of topics (order, inclusion/exclusion, etc.), the tone of the communication, the nature and location of any illustrations, and more, are among the many communication elements that can affect audiences. Even the type and placement of ads impact on readers'/listeners' understanding of content. In brief, it is not surprising that the mass media incite desires in people from even the most vigilant circles.

Unfortunately, the desires elicited by the mass media can make us baser than cows. I have yet to realize a bovine that covets its companion's hide. Daisy and Dalansky each seem content to chew their cud whether their coat is partially red, partially brown, or some other color. Likewise, I have yet to realize a cow that has real estate envy. Although certain demographics (namely, physical size; animals are called "brutes" for a reason) influence which individual, among a herd of cattle, is going to get preferential access to watering holes, to salt licks, and the like, once social status has been sorted out, most of those milk moms remain content with their place within their herd.

We humans operate differently than bovine. Spurred on by, but not necessarily catalyzed through, the mass media, lots of us share fantastic and immediate ideations about what we want and about what we ought to have. We remain confused about the difference between being modest and attractive to our husbands and being "up to date" on fashion (whereas white knee socks may not enhance matrimonial harmony, neither does investing in the opposite extreme of changing skirt fabrics, just because that trend has been lauded by ads. Such behavior can lead to debt as well as to a shutdown in Shalom Bayit.)

We remain confused about the difference between having a heimishe house open to guests and a striking house that is a more of a showplace than an environment for mitzvot (if the kids can't sit on the furniture and the guests can't use the dishes, then outside of the bathroom, where can people function normally?) We remain confused between maintaining our health and personally bankrolling the beauty industry (while it is laudable to treat bacterial and viral infections, it's unhealthy to obsess over lip color, gradations of notes in perfumes, or the emulsification temperature of hand creams.)

Certainly, the urge to conform (also called "low self-esteem" or "lack of b'tochen") and the urge to comply (also called "peer pressures" or "lack of emunah") contribute to our choices. Without the blinking, shiny, opulence presented by the mass media, perhaps we might be more like simple herbivores.

Our zeal, our servitude, is better directed toward Hashem than toward selecting fabrics, furnishings, and makeup. Until we are able to look through the mass media (whether or not we understand the devices at play), toward Shamayim, those cud chewers have one over us. Here, in the Holy Land, we need to release those temptations.

Brutality in the City: A Brief Response

The premeditated use of excessive force is not novel in the Middle East, nor, unfortunately is it unusual in Jerusalem, per se. However the massacre that took place on July 2, 2008, in the heart of this holy metropolis, at Mercaz HaRav Yeshiva, was nothing short of the most horrific offensive that a human being could perpetrate.

This allegedly spontaneous, independently executed occurrence, though, regrettably not a rarity among the cruelties suffered by our people, either in current times or during the course of our history, was an inestimable tragedy. Whenever a single individual, let alone multiple persons, are compelled to forfeit their lives, we can be confident that we are witnessing a cosmically-sanctioned disaster. On certain levels, catastrophes are not accidents.

We need to pray for the memory of those victims and for the health of the injured. We need to pray for and to enact our own behavioral revisals, too. Immediately.

My children were home when the news reached us. My husband was in another country, shepherding source code, as is his occupational responsibility. I was poking at my keyboard, busy with my own work.

I closed my most current window, left my office, and sought to survey the familial landscape. The scenery was grim. The kids, literally, were grief-stricken. Though they had heard and seen much in their comparatively short time in Israel, including, sadly, other enemy-precipitated losses of life, this most recent incident literally shocked them.

My children ride buses and walk around in the area where the carnage took place. It is getting increasingly difficult for them not to despair when we, Am Yisrael, are lead to slaughter by dint of our nation's internal or foreign policies or by other manner of political foolhardiness.

One by one, the little citizens in my life disbanded to the sanctuary of their respective rooms. A sleepover birthday party, a week of camping in the Golan, an awesome martial arts class, and an impending bagrout, respectively, suddenly seemed immaterial.

After scouring reliable news sources, acknowledging my children's feelings, and trying to make some sense out of the absurd, I, too, found myself silent. Although I usually wax expansive on many topics, I had little to offer to my offspring. What does one say in the face of murder?

Yoman, Day Planner, of a Mad Housewife

I am mad. Angry. Bitter. Upset. Aggrieved. I trust Hashem. I sure don't get what's going on.

When I woke up, shortly after 5 am the morning, after the horrific killings, i.e. the murders at Mercaz HaRav Yeshiva, in Kiryat Moshe, Missy Older, who otherwise would have been electronically hooking up with her New World friends, greeted me with a somber, "did you hear the news, Mommy?"

Mommy was barely awake. Yet, the news that eight humans, eight souls, eight people, were slaughtered at Mercaz HaRav Yeshiva jolted me like no other stimulant could. I sat for a few moments, after silently mouthing "Baruch Dayan HaEmet." I just sat.

Thereafter, I prayed Shacharit, but I prayed with the silence of a person shocked rather than with the joy of a person celebrating Rosh Chodesh Adar. I don't know what The Boss made from my prayers.

Thereafter, Missy Older and I woke up the younger children. Younger Dude said little as he sleepily grabbed a funky hat for his school's Rosh Chodesh Adar celebration. He wanted face paint, but I told him we wouldn't open that package until Purim. We told him nothing about the violence. There would be time.

As for Missy Younger, we told her slowly. First, we said one student was killed. She digested, with rancor, the news. After a necessary pause, she asked if others were dead. We told her of the seven other martyrs.

She digested, with further bad feeling, that news, too. Then, she asked, in a soft voice, where the killings had taken place. We told her in a neighborhood near her school.

Missy Younger's friend, who had slept over and who is a frequent fixture, Baruch Hashem, in our home, asked which yeshiva. We told her.

She told us that two of her brothers learn there. I gave her the phone and asked her to call her parents. I was relieved to know, b'li ayin hara, that her brothers were safe. I was horrified to think that someone else's brothers were not.

Madness knows no limits. Savagery makes no distinction.

While the girls were getting ready for school, I called a special friend. I nodded to the receiver as she reminded me that the world sees Jewish life as cheap and Israeli rights as nonexistent. It's easy for terrorists to take their cue from governmental brazenness.

Like a magician twirling one hand at his audience, all dazzle and flourish, while reaching with other into a secret compartment to actually release a lizard or rabbit, during the emptying of The Gush, the Israeli Government had already made concessions to the Road Map Plan. Is it such a surprise that the walls are falling?

Before we wished each other well, I asked my friend if I were wise to allow my daughter to travel to an outlying area for Shabbat. She pointed out that her own children settle hilltops and that I already knew what her answer would be. For a moment we laughed together, sharing a solidarity that is our love of this land and of its people.

I loaded Missy Younger and her pal into our car. They had grabbed chocolate cereal for breakfast, yet I had made no protest. They had also grabbed garish masks from our Purim stash and, again, I had made no complaint, having nothing in me upon which to draw.

After dropping off the girls, rather than return home to finish my Shabbat preparations or to work on a writing project, I went to the shuk. I needed to be with people. On route, I called more friends. I needed to hear their voices.

The shuk disappointed me, both literally and as a metaphor. It also confused me.

When I tried to engage some of the shopkeepers in talk about the previous night's events, they furtively indicated, by means of their eyes, their employees. My heart cried. Those Jews need their parnassah. They know that certain strata of our society provide less costly services than do others. Those Jews never heard my grandfather say that you get what you pay for.

Two of my shuk incidents were unlike the others, though. In one case, a very young man, who said he was just twelve, helped me haul a very heavy box to my car. He was all smiles, energy, and joy in living.

He confused me. He was not of my people, although he had not (yet) acquired the sneer, the squint, or the other elements of body language that so often accompany the "polite" discourse of Middle Easterners. When I thanked him for loading my box into my car, I meant it sincerely. I cannot hate innocence.

In another case, a shopkeeper, who had no employees of any nation, choosing, for whatever reason, to work alone, talked "on the level" with me. We shook our heads, we used words that touched our hearts and we allowed our eyes to brim with impossible feelings. He had no English and I have only a beggar's Hebrew, but we spoke a shared language.

I'm home now. I'm not sure if I want to keep my doctor's appointment in another part of the country since I travel there by a route on which there is a history of killings. It's Adar and all is upside down.

Raising Children while Vetting Israeli Politics

It almost makes sense to my offspring that their mama, concurrent with exuberantly celebrating our nation's existence and growth, can't manage to wax enthusiastic about some of its leaders. It's not that I consider the men and women, who make and enforce Israeli policy, as villains as much as it is that I am flummoxed by their ostensibly contradictory policies.

As an anxious consumer of news, I've noticed that my sources often cancel each other out. Whereas, my family's secure room is stocked and our gas masks are in position, B'ezrat Hashem, we ought never to need to use either of those types of safeties. Likewise, while I sometimes vote in elections, I am often surprised by "developments" in the parties in which I had confidence. What's more, there were certain cities as well as certain areas within cities, where I used to frequently drive, but given the recent removal of checkpoints, of barrier walls, and of other protections, I am no longer comfortable traveling.

At times, I am of the opinion that the Israeli public is getting victimized. Despite the fact that our government aims to conscript nearly all of our children, up to half of our earnings, and whichever of our homes it desires, that overseeing body denies many of us the right to bear arms at the same time that it trains its "regulators" to pounce on us. No, I'm not referring only to Yesha. Yes, I am angry.

Sure, one of my family's friends was a member of Jerusalem's City Council. Sure, one of our neighbor's sons still proudly serves in the city's police department. Sure, one of my own kids cites letter and verse that his rabbi instructed all students to obey command.

As well, I've been told that the double binds, which Israelis experience, are partially due to the multiple attempts, by the people in charge, to woo the support of "helper" nations. I've been advised that our sacred realm rubs its belly in the dust of international federations, sucks up clouds of anti-Semitic humiliation, and otherwise grovels before secular, narrow-minded groups so that Israel, on chance, might receive: fiduciary benefits, access to expensive military knowledge and equipment, and other "useful" extras.

There are at least three problems with our tolerance of this widespread behavior, discounting the craziness that such actions bring to the lives of us Israelis. First, the world *buys* Israeli knowhow and technology. Second, (political) prostitution can lead to disease, to disfigurement, and to death. Third, and most important, if we are chasing heads of state, we are neglecting to put Hashem in the equation.

That Israeli is an international leader in technology, in general, and in military applications, specifically, is easily documented. That political prostitution is a stupid policy, likewise, is easy to prove (click on most international news articles.) That we need, first and foremost, to look to G-d for protection, though, seems to need to be reiterated.

Hashem will not abandon His people. Granted, we have to make a sincere effort to do everything we can to protect ourselves. We need to make haste to inhabit Eretz Yisrael, specifically, and to be instrumental in creating our geulah, in general.

Nonetheless, ultimately, The Boss runs the show. We ought not to cleave to the latest and greatest social strategies, or the coattails of trendy politicians, but to the sanctity of Klal Yisrael and to our Maker. We recite, several times a day, the Shema. In that prayer, we reify our belief that The Almighty will protect us.

Yet, we continue recklessly, contenting ourselves with the "fact" that such metamagnetic transitions as the ones that our government imposes upon us, time and again, make some sort of convoluted sense. The media's views, which are repeatedly fed to us as so much pap, force themselves into our personal epistemologies.

Consequently, I'm unsure of how to respond to my sons and daughters. At the same time that I espouse words and enact deeds, all of which I hope witness my love for this Holy Land, for this Holy People, and for my love for Hakodesh Baruchu, I'm stymied when it comes to answering some of my children's insightful remarks. What does an Israeli parent say to her child, for instance, when that youth exclaims, with all due vigor, "in the next election, I'll be legal. I can choose among the liar, the hypocrite, and the thief."

Spies vs. Guides

Recently, Parsha Shelach Lecha, Send for Yourself, resonated with me in a way that made it worth remarking about during my family's three Shabbat *seudot*. Consequently, I interrupted my dear one's "regularly scheduled programming," their well-researched *drashot*, to give over some informal words on that section of Torah in which twelve of our nation's greatest leaders go to scout out Eretz Yisrael, but fail (except for two of them), to return with words of praise.

I ranted to my husband, to my sons, to my daughters, and to our guests, not so much about the downfall of those great men of that most superlative generation, but about the downfall of the rest of the Klal, e.g. about we whom received the spies' report with equanimity, rather than with indignation, and about we whom, subsequently, chose to rebel against our most precious leader, Moshe Rabbeinu. In addition, I groused about how our emancipated forefathers' participation in lashon hara serves as a warning to us not to repeat their deeds.

Sadly, many of us, akin to those ancestors of ours, who accepted the spies' report, are guilty both of listening to (as opposed to walking away from) defamatory speech about the Holy Land and of not championing her when she is lambasted (this second crime is more complex than the first crime since, in certain circumstances, objecting to words of lashon hara brings about additional levels and instances of lashon hara.) Specifically, we didn't and we still don't do enough to praise or to defend Eretz Yisrael.

One of the worst aspects of the original episode is that our nation, only a short time earlier, had witnessed the miracles at the Red Sea and at Har Sinai. Persons of such experiential lineage, who, additionally, escaped being sullied by having to continue to live among idolaters, dared to question Hashem's commands. Those lofty Jews sided with the spies rather than believing that when The Boss desires a certain outcome, i.e. that we ought to live in Eretz Yisrael, The Boss will make it happen no matter the difficulties that await us on route.

Interestingly, part of the problem with our backing the spies' malicious words about Eretz Yisrael was the doubt we used in referring to ourselves. Lashon hara does not only apply to words spoken about others, but also to the words we speak about us. In the case highlighted in Parsha Shelach Lecha, we believed our representatives were correct in considering us as nothing, as minutia akin to those found in the insect kingdom. Even if the spies had shared a truth, we ought not to have judged ourselves. It was never and will never be our lot to judge our own worth.

It is as bad for us to underappreciate our value as it is for us to live defiantly. We are just a bit lower than angels concurrent with being just a bit higher than dust. It's shortsighted, in the least, and morally wasteful, at the greatest, for us to use up our resources trying to figure out where, on the continuum of value, any of us sits.

If those faults were not enough, we also goofed when we tried to rectify the situation. Even secular, modern psychologists urge people to wait to apologize until any injured party is ready and willing to hear teshuva. To force reparations upon a victim is to pile hurt upon them.

Whereas The Almighty is in control of the universe and as such can't be victimized by us, G-d can be hurt by our choices. In the case of the break in our faith, which was displayed by our acting wayward in relationship to G-d's command to settle Israel, we compounded our error by trying to make our amends on our terms rather than per Hashem's strictures. Even though we were told it was no longer a good idea to try to conquer the Promised Land, some of us, wanting to be free of the nuisance of guilt, headed off anyway. Those persons, the ones among us, who insisted on "apologies" on their terms, were decimated. For a second time, those Jews acted according to their own program rather than in obedience.

As is hopefully apparent, the relevance of this Torah portion, for the status quo, is uncanny. Human might is not right and majority/quantitative consensus counts as truth only in rare census reports. While it most often remains too complicated for us to easily discern among would-be policy makers' agendas, it is essential for us to insist that we retain self-accountability.

Jews don't want, has v'shalom, to continue to be blameworthy because they created calumny against G-d. We want to live a life made secure through Hashem's abundant blessings. Period.

Like the Biblical spies, we modern Israelis fall off the path He established for us when we slander His land or His plan. At such times, we act from fear. We fear the real or imagined loss of status associated with "rolling up our sleeves and getting dirty," that is, with the business of advocating for Israel and for the goodness of dwelling here. It is common knowledge that privileged folk in Hutz L'Aretz, i.e. the rich and/or the professional, often find themselves earning their keep, after moving to Israel, by performing tedious work or by engaging in specialist activities for far less remuneration than they were accustomed.

Too often, professional training includes acculturating beginners to an attitude of entitlement, i.e. to the belief that professionals ought to expect to not have to think about, let alone have to actualize, "menial" labor. Yet, many contemporary, lauded rabbis, have been quoted as being happy, to literally be sweeping Israel's streets.

Furthermore, some of us modern day Jews fear losing our real or imagined social status when we join Jews ready to give up their lives to defend the honor and the turf that is our home. Said differently, some of us worry that if we are "caught" associating with "radicals," we will lose favor from other people. Ironically, at the end of our lives, that protected popularity will be meaningless, but our (lack of) helping to protect our land will be very significant.

Sadly, we repeat history in the disgrace we bring upon ourselves by doubting and failing to champion Hashem's design. We show ourselves to be ethically weak when we let our anxieties, instead of our emunah and our b'tochen, steer our lives. Rabbi Yitzchok Hecht stated, in his translation of the words of the two spies that praised Eretz Yisrael, Yehoshua and Kalev, that since Hashem is with us, there is no room for fear.[22]

---

22. Rabbi Yitzchok Hecht. "Yehoshus and Kalev." "Weekly Dvar Torah." *National Council of Young Israel.* 17 June, 2017. http://www.yihillcrest.org/Parsha/Shelach2017.pdf.

Communication Climate, Incommensurability, and Relationships

Communication climate is the social tone concurrently emerging from and contextualizing a relationship. This tone can be understood as being particularly "hostile," as being particularly "friendly," as being "neutral," or as being any one of the many other points along the hostile/friendly continuum.

Since communication climate is generated by communicators, behaviors which lend themselves to community building in one situation may break a community in another. This certainty holds for both communication emerging from socially-generated norms (top-down communication) and for communication emerging from individually-reinforced norms (bottoms-up communication).

For example, along the streets of Mea Shearim, in Jerusalem, an individual failing to aid a fallen citizen might be disdained as a person who: pays no attention to the needs of others, is unfeeling, is irresponsible, or is socially inept. However, an individual failing to aid a fallen citizen in another culture, e.g. in New York City, might be lauded as a person who: protects himself, is wise, is savvy, is street-smart, or is otherwise socially astute.

Another example of how culture can impact individual mores is the Israeli doctor whose first words to a new patient are "why are you so fat?" That medical professional boasts long lines of eager clients and is festooned with great accolades by her peers. No one questions her curt demeanor; her presentation of self is considered de rigor among Old Worlders. However, if that same doctor were to practice medicine in that way in The New World, she: would have few patients, would be disabused of her reputation by her peers, might get sued, and, if continually verbally "abusive," might even loose her license.

A third example of collective standard's impact on individual ethics is represented by the Israeli penchant for introducing questions into conversations, the nature of which, in the least, would be considered rude by New Worlders. Many olim have been amazed by Israelis' habit of asking how much olim earn, what olim homes cost, why olim pray at one synagogue and not another, and so forth.

As amazing as is Israeli culture's ability to influence individuals' communication norms, equally amazing is individual Israelis' abilities to influence Israeli society. Whereas in The New World, bottoms-up communication prevents people from squeezing the fruit, from talking in theatres, or from spitting on a sidewalk (all of which are informally sanctioned acts, here), in the Old World, bottoms-up communication reinforces such behaviors as: keeping infants that are left in trams in hallways or outside of stores, safe; preventing house guests from devolving into "royalty" (in The Old World, be prepared to wash dishes, sweep under tables, or serve if you are invited to visit someone), and dissuading strangers from walking off with soccer balls or dolls left in a park or on a stoop.

These ideas about the function of top-down communication on individual ethics and about the function of bottoms-up communication on social ethics are not new, yet, they establish needed premises for this essay.

Consider that if a New Worlder and an Old Worlder join in marriage, there will be "temperature regulation" issues. Consider that if people from two different cultures join in peace talks, there will be "temperature regulation" issues.

Literally, if an oleh from the Northeast seaboard of North America marries a native of Tel Aviv, the two will disagree on the meaning of "hot" and of "cold." The New Worlder, accustomed to Sukkot seasons bringing feet, not inches, of snow, will equate "cold" with temperature worthy of: chains on tires, goose down comforters, equipping cars with flashlights and kitty litter (the former in case of getting stuck in the ice and snow, the latter to provide traction to get out of the ice and snow) wool sweaters, leggings beneath skirts and pants, and double layers of mittens. Such an individual would regard most Israeli winters as relatively "balmy."

That person's Israeli spouse, on the other hand, accustomed to Sukkot seasons bringing rain and temperatures no longer capable of melting lizards or of sending hedgehogs running for shade, will equate "cold" with the need to unbox winter weight scarves and gloves, and the need to turn on the heat (I admit I have not yet gotten accustomed to the sight of so many Israelis wrapped, at least around their necks and wrists, as though a blizzard was coming. It still looks funny to my New World eyes to see folk strolling in a combination of light jackets and ear muffs.) Such an individual would position most Israeli winters as "uncomfortably cold." The two spouses, therefore, would be likely to experience much "temperature" while sparring over "heat."

Similarly, individuals from two different cultures have different notions about "national priorities." Jews value human life. We are willing to release thousands of prisoners for the reciprocal release of an individual or for a handful of individuals, to give away sacred land for peace, and to destroy our people's homes and neighborhoods to stop killings.

Terrorists, on the other hand, value regional dominion. They are willing to sacrifice young children and women, and to forfeit their lives, for their cause. They readily use civilians as shields and frequently threaten to destroy the entire Middle East, their people included, in the name of destroying anyone they hate.

The problem that the Old/New World couple encounters and that the people from the differing cultures encounter is an inability to understand, not merely semantically, but, more so, psychologically and socially, what "cold" or what "the value of a life" means to each other. Incommensurate communication is truly more complex than deciding if a friend is a one cheek (New World) or a two cheek (Old World) kisser or whether or not one should gently or forcibly remove lizards from one's bathtub.

Knowing how to respond to matters in which participants' sensibilities evolve from very different collectives is knowledge usually rewarded by "perfect" marriages or by Nobel Peace Prizes. It is improbable that one can successfully bridge such disparities, i.e. can create a system of understanding that is sufficiently encompassing to validate two divergent systems and that makes sense.

If "incommensurability" were merely a matter of people "talking past each other," we could get rid of the "irreconcilable differences" category for divorce and Israel could enjoy lasting peace with her neighbors. The Boston dude and his Tel Aviv bride could be compassionate, albeit not empathetic, about each other's childhood experiences of Sukkot season weather. Israel's neighbors could agree with her on the number of kilometers that she holds from the Dead Sea to the Red Sea and on solutions to mutual water use problems.

Unfortunately, the man from Boston and his wife from Tel Aviv, like Israel and her neighbors, are "counting" via different systems. Some are reckoning temperature via a measuring cup and others are reckoning using a barometer. To suggest that the Boston dude reach for Shalom Bayit by wearing summer weight clothes while his spouse jacks up the heat or that the Tel Aviv lady endure an icy apartment because her spouse is "confused" about seasons is absurd. Likewise, giving away yet another settlement or allowing outside interests to determine Israel's economic policy, too, makes little sense.

So, resentment builds. Cycles perpetuate. Marriages shatter. War ensues. Communication climates become hostile and breed further hostility in communicators.

There are possible responses (as opposed to "solutions;" the notion of "solutions" assumes diametrically opposed behaviors, not diametrically opposed understandings of behavior) to these signification conundrums. No response works all of the time - certain communication incommensurabilities are extremely difficult to resolve (we still await the peace that will surround Moshiach.)

One possible response to communication incommensurabilities is acknowledging, rather than evaluating, conflicting value systems. Although such an approach does not resolve, per se, undergirding differences, it helps to move martial communicators from a "hostile" stance toward a "friendly" one. This tactic is employed by both marriage counselors and peace negotiators.

In the case of the couple with different sensibilities about "appropriate" Sukkot season apartment temperature, the spouses' respective life experiences could be acknowledged and their dissimilar needs for heat, too, could be granted. In the case of the warring nations, their dissimilar meanings for "the value of a life" could be recognized and their dissimilar claims to land "being honored," too, could be recognized.

Per the couple, peace might be forthcoming after the communication climate of their marriage thaws; once the two become more comfortable speaking to each other, they might birth their own creative solution to their dilemma. Metacommunication has repeatedly proved itself successful in moving discourse from a place of breakdown to a place at which parties are receptive to an array of solutions. As for the warring nations, history has shown that "speaking politely," i.e. within mutually understood conventions, is insufficient to stop military crusades. If total annihilation of one's enemy, even at the cost of the entirety of one's people, is part of one party's core beliefs, there is no room for sincere negotiations.

Fortunately, there exist other responses to communication incommensurabilities, beyond thawing the communication climate. In situations in which conceding value systems fails, finding common denominators sometimes succeeds (and sometimes not; consider the classic move of staying in a highly dysfunctional marriage "for the sake of the children.") "Finding common communication denominators" means "finding beliefs which neither party holds as vital" or "illuminating beliefs that both parties, unbeknownst to themselves, hold in common." In the first case, this approach could mean identifying that the dude from Boston doesn't care whether his apartment is heated with oil or with solar power and that his Tel Aviv wife doesn't care if heat loss is compensated for with extra clothes or with extra blankets. The illumination of such seemingly microscopic points of negotiation, in turn, can provide jumping off points for additional concessions.

In the case of the warring nations, finding a common denominator could mean revealing areas of mutual "flexibility." Rhetorical analysis, for instance, might reveal that no Middle Eastern power broker cares if, G-d forbid, the region goes nuclear, that none of Israel's neighbors care if she is, G-d forbid, is decimated via homicide bombers or via nukes, and

Israel not caring whether she is defended by conventional arms or by nukes. In such a scenario, there is an agreement about the acceptability of nuclear arms. Plus, both Israeli and her neighbors believe they have a preordained right to a certain sliver of real estate. On two points, similar beliefs have been uncovered. Such a tactic can move combatants away from discourse incommensurabilities (but not necessarily from domestic or political stalemate).

A third way to overcome incommensurability is to impose a new value system on the involved parties. Sometimes this works (whether through suasory or coercive rhetoric) and sometimes it does not. People still get divorced. Economic sanctions and military displays fail. Even if a new, all-embracing, system of meaning does not: invalidate, bind in paradoxes, or otherwise minimalize communicators' core beliefs, it has the power to create a hierarchy of ends that can subsume communicators' prior epistemologies. The trouble is that communicators sometimes hold their core beliefs as more precious than peace.

Whereas the married couple might value their harmony over giving up temperature control and, as a result, might be willing to work "for the greater good" of their union, they might as likely be stuck in a need to be "correct," and, as a result, refuse to budge no matter the increase in their marital conflict. In terms of the warring nations, similarly, if both are willing to accept a "bigger," mutual, system of values, they can make peace. Otherwise, their choices remain unilateral concession or war.

Sometimes, it is not the communicators that are stuck at an impasse - outsiders, too, might be culpable for communicators' inability to make peace. Intervention by a third party, such as a rabbi or counselor, or such as an international intermediary, might prove inept, or for some other, e.g. socially-sanctioned "reason," arbitrators might be perceived, by one or both of the feuding parties, as delegitimate.

No response to communication incommensurabilities always works. Nonetheless, given the importance of concord, among individuals, and among nations, we need to attempt to remove hostility from our communication climates.

Media Serpents

Something that's fascinating to consider is that political perfume is often employed not to enhance a good scent, but to mask a vile one. In this case, I am referring to the media machinations of the 45th Vice President of the United States, of the man who served under President Bill Clinton and who fought in Vietnam; I am referring to the spin doctoring issued by Al Gore around a questionable profit he realized.

Specifically, that former USA Vice President, who sold his American media outlet, Current TV, to Al Jazeera, for an estimated half of a billion dollars, and who took home roughly one hundred million from that deal, covered his moral culpability, that is, rationalized his creation of yet another avenue for the communication of terror, by claiming that he "wanted to make the world a better place." That man, himself a Nobel Peace Prize winner, and former senator, who had stood staunchly with the political minority that supported the Gulf War, seemed more interested in riches than in improving international politics.

Mr. Gore knew that Al Jazeera "held an on-air birthday party a few years ago for the notorious Palestine Liberation Front terrorist Samir Kuntar who kidnapped and brutally murdered a Jewish man and his four-year old daughter ."[23] Mr. Gore most likely realized, too, that Al Jazeera continues on with its dubious intentions, and that it is the network that aired, "during the height of the war on terror… smuggled videos of Osama bin Laden."[24] It doesn't take rocket science to grasp that Al Jeezara is a Qatar-funded

23. Ari Davidson. "Prime-Time Jihad." *Breslov.co.il.* http://www.breslev.co.il/article-PrintVersion.aspx?id=23927&language=hebrew.

24. Howard Kurtz. "Why Al Gore's Al Jazeera Deal Doesn't Seem Right." *CNN.com.* 7 Jan., 2013. http://edition.cnn.com/2013/01/07/opinion/kurtz-gore-al-jazeera/index.html.

news agency and friend to Hamas. Nonetheless, the former Vice President of the United States sold his bandwidth to Sheikh Hamad bin Khalifa Al Thani, Emir of Qatar.

Ironically, Mr. Gore considers himself a person of principles. Gore had had "an offer from Glenn Beck to buy Current TV, but … turned it down out of hand on the grounds that the two were philosophically incompatible. He had no such qualms[, though,] about pocketing $100 million from the Qatar-owned propaganda outlet for America's terrorist enemies."[25] It seems that "when Glen Beck's far-right program, *The Blaze*, approached *Current TV* with an interest in purchasing them last year, they were reportedly told that ['] the legacy of who the network goes to is important to us and we are sensitive to networks not aligned with our point of view. ['] Besides, selling to fossil fuel-financed *Al Jazeera*, which apparently is much more aligned with *Current's* philosophy, probably provided a lot more green."[26]

Media pundits' jabs aside, think about the problem inherent in helping to broadcast the ideals of jihad-intent Islamists. If your imagination is stuck, refer to the massacre at the Boston Marathon and to the letters, mailed to Mississippi Senator Roger Wicker and to President Obama, which tested positive for ricin.

It's less than funny that world-wizened Mr. Gore seems unable to recognize: why unbalanced coverage of Israel and of the USA is problematic, why provocative rhetoric spurs fighting as well as calls up individual acts of violence, and why aiding the hijacking of popular culture, by people who hate what is good and just, makes him, at best, a fool, and at worst, a traitor. "Every time that you see a wounded member of the American military, or attend a service for those who died defending America, there is the distinct possibility that the death and destruction was carried out by Jihadists egged on by Al Jazeera. [B]oth Al Jazeera Arabic and Al Jazeera

---

25. Ben Shapiro. "Current TV Bought by Al Jazeera." *Frontpagemag.com.* 10 Jan., 2013. http://www.frontpagemag.com/fpm/172939/current-tv-bought-al-jazeera-ben-shapiro.

26. Larry Bell. "Al Gore's Oil-Fueled Al Jazeera Deal Follows A String Of Green Energy Fiascos." *Forbes.* Jan 8, 2013. https://www.forbes.com/sites/larrybell/2013/01/08/al-gores-oil-fueled-al-jazeera-deal-follows-a-string-of-green-energy-fiascos/#3600f881369e.

English [are] considered outlets for al-Qaeda propaganda messages."[27] Few people would contest that Islamists: desire, G-d Forbid, the obliteration of Israel, use children as human shields and as combatants, are more interested in conquest than in peace, and employ any means available to them, no matter how morally corrupt those means are, to achieve their ends. Simple, Al Jazeera is a tool of terrorism.

Sure, the Al Jeezera website claims that "the introduction of Al Jazeera into American homes can only offer a competitive advantage in a highly networked world that is fractured yet very fluid."[28] Nonetheless, folk with half of a brain will look at those words as specious.

Most of us do not try to "prove our machismo" by eating fugu, puffer fish, or by lining our pockets with the profits of such sales. We scorn blood money and avoid associating with things that are known poisons. Most of us are not Al Gore.

----

27. Cliff Kinkaid. "Congress Fails to Act Against Gore's Terror TV Deal." *American Survival News.* 31 Jan., 2013. http://www.usasurvival.org/home/ck01.31.13.html#axzz-4pANiq23w.

28. Dinesh Sharma. "Cultural Diffusion in the American News Media." *aljeezera.com.* 14 Jan., 2013. http://www.aljazeera.com/indepth/opinion/2013/01/2013114111510648291.html.

An Ongoing Crisis

On the one hand, we are related to Ishmael. His descendants, in times of clarity, celebrate this connection. Consider Iraqi poet Alaa Alsaegh's work, "Cries from the Heart of the Holocaust," posted on *Arabs for Israel*.[29] On the other hand, those same ethnic cousins are ferocious in their reaction to any self-declared friend of the Jews. Alaa Alsaegh, in broad daylight, in a populous American city, was attacked by Muslim men and was mutilated for his act of sympathizing with us.[30] Brotherly love that ain't.

Hatred of Jews, anti-Semitism (anti-Zionism), is woven into the social agendas of many nations. Muslim politicos, alongside of contemporary leaders of Islam, decry Israel's existence. As well, even those world denizens, who don't support extremes, turn a blind eye to language promoting such loathing. Nonie Darwish writes in "Why Muslims Must Hate the Jews," posted on *American Thinker*, that "it is at the heart of Islamic theology that world peace will be established only when all the Jews are wiped from the earth. But few people in Western media are alarmed by this kind of rhetoric or care to expose this dreadful dark side of Islam's obsession with Jew hatred."[31]

---

29. Alaa Alsaegh. "Cries from the Heart of the Holocaust." *Arabs for Israel*. 27 Sept., 2011. http://arabsforisrael. blogspot.co.il/2011/09/poem-by-iraqi-poet-alaa-alsaegh. html.

30. Pat Franklin. "Wonders of Islam: Muslims attack Christian convert in broad daylight in St Louis and carve the Star of David on his back [sic]." *The Free Press*. 31 Nov., 2011. http://www.thefreepressonline.co.uk/news_print/1/2334.htm.

31. Nonie Darwish. "Why Muslims Must Hate the Jews." *American Thinker.com*. 3 Aug., 2012.http://www.americanthinker.com/articles/2012/08/why_muslims_must_hate_ jews.html.

Regard the values iconicized in poetry fashioned by other Arab poets and regard the world's reaction to those texts, Itamar Marcus and Nan Jacques Zilberdik report in "EU-funded Palestinian NGO Glorifies Hijackings, Terror, and Hatred of Israel and the US," posted on *Palestinian Media*

Watch, that much discourse emanating from the Middle East glorifies plane hijackings and threatens Israel and the United States. In venues such as Palestinian Authority TV programs for youth, i.e. in *Speak Up*, teenage hosts encourage Arab teens to engage in acts of violence and remind them that they can do so with impunity. Marcus and Zilberdik surmise that "European countries, the UN and other well-intentioned donors [that] fund programs that seem to be positive for Palestinian youth, [fail to realize that] these programs glorify terrorists or promote hatred."[32]

Despite the awfulness of sword-waving Arab rhetoricians and despite the thoughtlessness of the international community that funds them, the biggest component of our ongoing crisis of hatred is neither our inability to "work peaceably" with other Semites nor the global population's casting off of its responsibilities to Israel. Historically, we have been an unloved, much maligned people, who have survived many hostile regimes, even thrived, because of the help of Hashem.

Today, however, it seems as though we are less wonderful because our primary directive has been largely discarded by us. We don't act as though we care about ourselves. Mull over the fact that in 2012, when we were being targeted by enemy ballistics, our convergent media rang with calls to arm and with words of bravery. Not so, today.

Words are cheap. Low-cost items get quickly thrust aside. Our news now is of the Jewish child gunned down in Connecticut and of the forthcoming national elections in Israel. Somehow, very quickly, we have managed to drop the imperative topic of our continued existence.

---

32. Itamar Marcus and Nan Jacques Zilberdik. "EU-funded Palestinian NGO Glorifies Hijackings, Terror, and Hatred of Israel and the US." *Palestinian Media Watch*. 20 Dec., 2012. http://palwatch.org/main.aspx?fi=157&doc_id=8219.

Caryn Lipson suggests in "This is My Territory," posted on *In A Good Place Thoughts about Life in The Holy Land*, that whereas "[w]hen one talks about being American, Canadian, Israeli, British, Ethiopian, Russian, etc., it's very often a cultural identification, rather than a geographic one,"[33] when one talks about being Israel, it is both a cultural and a geographic naming.

We are Am Yisrael. Eretz Yisrael is our Jewish Home. We are more than grievously negligent when we forget the significance of making self-preservation first and foremost in our hearts, in our mind, and in our media. It is up to us to deal with our ethnic relatives' aggressions, to stand up to their assaults. We must not minimalize any hostility whether those acts are comprised of words or of blood.

As expressed in "Israel: The Holy Land," on *Chabad.org*, "[f]or a Jew, the Land of Israel is more than a place. It is a body for the soul of a people. As Yom Kippur is to the Jewish year, so Israel is to the Jewish space: a place to find where you began, where you belong and what you truly are. A Jew does not travel to Israel, but returns there."[34] A Jew making aliyah does not merely buy an apartment in Tel Aviv or merely enroll in a school in Beer Sheva; he or she subsumes Jewish history into his or her daily life. This way of being is a verity, not a choice.

Not only must we integrate an awareness of the nature of the Jewish people and the Jewish land into our personal and collective selves, but we must, as well, defy global pressure to stop developing self-love. That is, we must build up our roads, our schools, and our villages. We must defend our land. We must insist on the safety of all of our dear ones (A parsimonious take on this matter is given in the wonderful, animated YouTube Video, "Terror in School," produced by the group Scratch, "in response to the ongoing Israeli-Palestinian conflict.")[35]

---

33. Caryn Lipson. "This is My Territory." *In A Good Place: Thoughts about Life in The Holy Land.* 24 July, 2011. https://bimakomtov.wordpress.com/?s=this+is+my+territory.

34. "Israel: The Holy Land." *Chabad.org.* http://www.chabad.org/library/article_cdo/aid/588018/jewish/Israel.htm.

35. Scratch. "Terror in School." YouTube. 28 Nov., 2012. https://www.youtube.com/watch?v=Cbdnu_R9G40.

To be Jewish is to protect our Jewish Homeland. To be Jewish is to back Jews. "Eliora" writes in "A Gap-Year Student: I Took Peace for Granted," posted on the Facebook page, *Stop the Rockets: Social Task Force for Israel,* that she never imagined she would be in jeopardy.[36] Yet, she was. We are. As long as we are more afraid of what other nations and persons think of us, and as long as we are guilty of focusing on keeping up, socially, economically, or otherwise, with the real or imagined people in our lives, and as long as we fail to make Israel the most important of our concerns, we are in danger.

The continuity of Judaism requires us to secure ourselves now, completely. Our cousins treat us brutally. The rest of the world, at best, is apathetic about our cause. We must manifest focus on our survival, and, in partnership with The Boss, buttress ourselves. Now. Immediately. Forever.

---

36. "Eliora." "A Gap-Year Student: I Took Peace for Granted." *Stop the Rockets: Social Task Force for Israel. Facebook.* 2012.

Media Savvy: The Fires of Rhetoric

In an ordinary neighborhood, one that is important to the people that live there, a house is burning. The family that owns the house has escaped and is safe. The building, however, continues to burn. Someone driving through the neighborhood notices the fire. She looks for a phone from which she can call other people to help her extinguish it. She is a firefighter.

The fire is eventual put out. The damage to the house is substantial, but the house is reparable. The family will suffer inconveniences, but has been spared permanent loss.

Several weeks pass. The family thanks the fire company for its services.

Several years pass. The fire company, again, "hears" from the family. Another fire has burned the family's house. This time, though, the fire killed the family and destroyed the building. Ironically, the second fire had the same cause as the first. Yet, the family failed to heed the firefighters' warnings.

In a second neighborhood, one that is also important to its residents, a different fire is burning. Stop. Trade "neighborhood fire" and "family home burning" for "media bias against Israel" and for "rhetorical bias against a select segment of the Jewish population."

Let's get started. Israel/a select segment of the Jewish population has been slandered, but has escaped and is safe, while the symbols that sheltered her/them continue to burn. Someone alert to media content notices the fire. That aware individual looks for a means to connect to some people to help him or her extinguish the blaze that he or she noticed since he or she is a media professional.

The fire is eventual put out. The damage to Israel/a select segment of the Jewish population is substantial, but reparable. Israel/a select segment of the Jewish population suffers inconveniences, but is spared permanent loss. Several weeks pass. Israel/a select segment of the Jewish population thanks the media practitioners and the attendant scholars.

Several years pass. The professionals "hear" from Israel/a select segment of the Jewish population, again. Another fire has burned their symbol system. This time, though, the slander killed their repute and totally decimated the emblems that sheltered them. Ironically, the second incident had the same cause as the first. Yet, the victims failed to heed the professionals' warnings.

Slander and its sister, libel, are only a few of the social conflagrations that media professionals fight. Prejudice, ignorance, fear, and greed also fuel many fires. Usually, though, "neighbors" do little to help firefighters combat disasters. Instead, neighbors rely on firefighters to protect whom or what they love.

"Neighbors" often also claim that they maintain fireproofed private "properties," including: their personal libraries, computer networks, and schools' newspapers; and maintain fireproofed public "properties" such as speech rights acts, e.g. the First and Fifth Amendments. Yet, recent disasters, such as the censoring of high school newspapers, such as Congress's ruling on the Freedom of Information Act, and such as the Meese Commission's conclusions on pornography, invalidate this claim.

Consequently, a major responsibility of firefighters remains educating the public, helping them prevent new fires. Our brave protectors have to repeatedly emphasize the interdependence of individuals' social safety. Sometimes, "neighbors" respond to firefighters' efforts superficially; they bestow privileges and honors upon those professionals. At such times, media scholars and practitioners are given: celebrity status, tenure, scientific prizes, or government ranks.

Other times, "neighbors" respond to firefighters' efforts substantively; they engage in the preventions encouraged by them. At such times, "neighbors:" hold forums on social issues, demand that reading skills are stressed, or question the priorities of the media (firefighters, too, are susceptible to graft). Most of the time, though, "neighbors" do not apply themselves to the business of social safety or entirely deny media professionals' fears. It is easier for "neighbors" to blame firefighters for unsalvageable symbol systems than to take responsibility for those systems, themselves.

Fortunately, Israel/select segments of the Jewish population's lack of concern for the warnings from, their roadblocks to the progress made by, and their stigmatizing of media professionals, do not ordinarily deter the firefighting. It is not that the firefighters are more virtuous than are "neighbors" as many firefighters fear fires, and suffer from their own kinds of apathy, as it is that firefighters' knowledge and experience tell them that the blaze they fail to respond to might be the one that consumes the persons or things they love.

In view of that, it remains vital that Israel and that all segments of the Jewish population become aware of, and, sometimes, act on the ideas of media spokespersons, of social critics, and of researchers. What's more, Israel and all segments of the Jewish population ought to have a conceptual command of human rules, which incorporate the relevancy of the measures of "goodness," of "fairness," and of "virtue." Israel and all segments of the Jewish population should, as well, work to possess more than inklings about the relationships of individuals to society, of society to the media, and of the media to governance.

As long as we remain "victims" or "neighbors of victims," we fail to: provide role models, emphasize the social importance of communication skills and knowledge, illustrate the relationship of mediated communication to the shaping of social knowledge, in general, and to the questioning of communication sources, specifically. We might as well be supplying the matches. Mt. Carmel went up in a blaze, recently. Much "news" about Israel, and about Jews, too, has unnecessarily been set aflame.

International Media Phubar: Rhetorically Guarding our Homeland

From horrendous headlines to content made of blather, the media remain unrelentingly anti-Semitic, hence unrelentingly anti-Israel. It's not so much an "Arab Spring" or the Palestinian Movement's proposed UN do-si-do, with which we have to be concerned, but with sloppy reporting and with sloppy consumption of ideas.

In no small part, by dint of questionable "witnessing," our enemies have succeeded in whittling away our land and in otherwise denuding our heritage. Consider the lack of careful reporting on the March, 2011 Itamar Massacre. Consider the world's focus not on the actual murders near Eilat, but on the probable loss of material goods in Washington and in New York.

The "proper"' roles for government and for the media get muddled time and again as heads of state look for favorable election results and as heads of broadcast agencies look for gold, for silver, and for other sources of revenue. Although Israel remains democracy's best Middle Eastern ally, leaders seem willing to cash in on the immediate gratification of access to an uninterrupted flow of oil and willing to cash in on the ability to place correspondents in risky regions, rather than to seek truth, justice, or old-fashioned authenticity.

Mighty nations have repeatedly asked Israel to defer defending herself and have asked her to cede components of her sovereignty. Those countries' heads even publically admit that they care more for their pockets than they do for the Jewish homeland. Yet, their ill-advised machinations and the motives behind such ill-advised deeds frequently go unreported in the media.

Just as Sino fashion, food, and folklore became popular during the Nixon administration, in no small part as a means of retooling common thought about specific international relations; these days, Arab fashion, food and folklore have become the frenzied choice of the media. It's not accidental that, for example, *The New York Times*, over the last decade, has featured more Arab-friendly language and images on its front page than it had in all of its previous decades, combined, or that the publication has engaged in increasing numbers of acts of Jew bashing. Likewise, it ought to surprise no one that, for several seasons, the Canadian Broadcasting Corporation has co-opted Laura Ingalls Wilder's books about family values, about love, about friendship, and about faith, presenting them as an ethical mash known as *Little Mosque on the Prairie*. As long as it's lucrative and trendy to use media channels to wallop Israel, few media gatekeepers or agencies that observe the media, protest bias accounts.

This dilemma, moreover, leads to a second problem; few citizens question the pabulum fed to them by news outlets. Consequently, politicians rabidly hostile to Jewish needs get reelected and public sources of information that glower with anti-Semitism get reified for repeated communications. Pack journalism, questionable media research, and biased reporting, i.e. unethical media practices, get intertwined with motives of government and of publics in ways that shore up the additional problems of unethical international policy and of unethical citizen responses to global issues.

It seems as though no one cares any longer about the confusion of "proper" notions of policy and freedom with inflated ones. The passing on of news and of other information continues to disintegrate. People assimilate more and more balderdash.

Even when other nations are willing to allow their social and moral duties to slide, Israel cannot afford to do so. Halakah forbids us from relying on miracles. Just as the Temple will not fall from the sky, i.e. we have to help build it, we cannot and ought not to wait for benevolent social channels to speak well of our land and of our people.

Beyond groups like the Jewish Internet Defense Force and Hasbara, it behooves us to back or, better yet, to actively participate in, small and large efforts to disseminate favorable information about Jews and about Israel. Language matters.

By placing our thoughts front and center in the world media, we can define ourselves. It is far more important, after all, that we assume our duty in describing "Israel," and in delineating "Jewishness" than it is for us to guarantee that the price of gasoline remains "affordable." Even when international presses remain in a phubar state, we can rhetorically guard our land and our sanctity.

Communication Rules

A bottoms-up approach to explaining the rules of ritualized discourse allows for the negotiated assignment of meaning to life events. By assigning significance to our experiences, per interpretations favored by the populous, as opposed to by interpretations favored by the elite, we are subjecting ourselves to a broad-based give and take. Such a strategy is good when talking to Knesset members, to assistant bank managers, to Jerusalem cabbies, and to small (and not-so-small) children.

For instance, since the majority of religious Jews, who hire cabs in Jerusalem, do not own cars and do care about the conduct of their drivers, their emotional investment in their drivers' decorum impacts Jerusalem cabbies' behavioral norms. Simply, many Jerusalem cabbies cover their heads. Most cabbies likewise are familiar with quick, inexpensive routes to religious places. The majority of cabbies, too, know not to hand money to, or to take money directly from, religious women's hands. In a word, the religious population's ongoing reinforcement of certain ways of acting has regulated the actions of the city's cab drivers more than has top-down legislation.

Likewise, my children's consistent, predictable behavior around preparing Shabbat meals has influenced my behavior more than have family meetings on the matter. Specifically, when my children, as aided by the Computer Cowboy, invite me to tend to other matters while they cook for Shabbat, there are certain norms that I can expect will be fulfilled (which is why this mother does the majority of her family's food preparation).

Particularly, when the kids cook, I am not allowed to comment on the state of the kitchen (unless they totally forget to clean up), on the items on the "menu" (unless the wee ones buy soda), or on the amount of convenient or contrived dishes used (Since I'm a Jewish Mother, I use lots of fruits and vegetables in my preparations - I don't want my babies to be missing essential vitamins or minerals.) My children, on the other hand, see "successful cooking" as cooking that requires the fewest possible number of vessels to clean. Their food tastes great, but with their creations are almost always missing bioflavonoids. Like it or not, I yield, since my family's majority has declared that if I forgo the work, I likewise forgo the right to establish behavioral constraints around that work. Confusing.

Granted, hiring a cab is as mundane an act as cooking (although either of these behaviors could lead to something sacred.) Cabs can be hired to go to the Kotel, to get to kollel, or to attend a shiur. People can cook in honor of Shabbat, for a holiday, or for a seudah. That said, bottoms-up influences on individuals' understanding of social rules can occur during sacred moments, too. Take, for example, this year's Mo'ed Sukkah celebration of Birkat Kohanim at The Kotel.

Consider the way in which the crowd attending Shacharit and Mussaf exited the old city. The people leaving prayers did not depart the venue in an ordinary fashion, i.e. in a fashion dictated by tradition, which was influenced by rabbanim. Rather, the crowd left in a fashion governed by their sensibilities.

During that particular Mo'ed Sukkah morning, durng which I merited to be a witness, the Kotel's courtyard overflowed; with many tallisim-bedecked Kohanim, plus large numbers of foreign Jews praying, in many languages, to The Boss. There were locals in attendance, too. The texture of that congregation was different than the texture of worshippers whom pray at The Kotel on most weekday afternoons. Yet, it was that difference that colored the congregation's leave from the Kotel.

Whereas cell phones were flicked open and cigarettes were lit a respectable distance from the prayer site, and whereas strains of English, French, Russian, Spanish, German, and other tongues were detectable in a higher concentration than on a typical day, some manifestations of that group's leave-taking were notably uncharacteristic for Israel. It was not the worshippers whom lingered, adding paragraphs of *Tehillim* to their prayers or otherwise asking Hashem for mercy and grace, nor the quieter worshippers whom sat in rows a little back from the ancient stones, who impacted the difference, but the worshippers who were already heading toward public transportation that were remarkable. In a word, few of those Jews rushed.

The buses spilled over with people who had come and prayed, who gave up their seats to elders. Also, rather than pushing, the people in the cab queues were orderly. Less shoving than normal occurred on the Old City's narrow streets, too. That is to say, the public's interpretation of the norms for exiting the holy site were aberrations of daily conduct (we should be so lucky as to experience such "aberrations" on a regular basis.)

In addition, many of those visiting Jews lingered in the Old City. The enterprises lining the walkways to and from the holiest place on earth were filled beyond capacity with Jews suddenly needing falafel or bagels. Students sat on stones sipping cola (they have more liberal mothers that do my children), grandparents fed grandbabies, college-aged kids sang lovely melodies. People eased into their days instead of rushing, Israeli-style, to get to their next appointment.

Although it's possible that the partial holiday nature of Mo'ed influenced the actions of the crowd, I think otherwise. I believe that when large numbers of Jews get together, we positively influence each other. It is incumbent upon us to make holy choices regularly, so I would like to believe, suitably, that the members of the vast group, who were praying at the Kotel that morning (newspapers reported thousands in attendance) positively influenced each other and that the results of such influence were independent of any group members' formal learning.

Just a few weeks later, when I returned to the Kotel, it was "business of usual." Local ethnics were aggressive in their economic pursuit of tourists and locals alike (disregarding that visibly identifiable religious Jews would have no interest in nonkosher food products) and Jews, who were fewer in number than during the past semi-holiday, were a bit too preoccupied to realize that the old man, whom they had pushed in front of to board a bus, struggled with a loaded shopping cart, or that the young woman, whom they had shoved to catch a cab, walked with a leg brace.

Likewise, even more few weeks after the public Priestly Blessing, when the excitement of the holidays was over, Missy Older, Older Dude, Missy Younger, and Younger Dude, as aided by Computer Cowboy, again offered to prepare our family's Shabbat meals. Whereas the children conceded cola, they insisted that their cooking include French fries. The power of bottoms-up communication rules endures.

I Will Not Forget Thee, O Jerusalem!

Adar is a month of madness, of masks, and of threats of genocide to the Jewish People. Fortunately, Adar is also a month of emunah, of exposing fraud, and of our redemption. How an individual experiences this month depends on how he or she lives.

Sadly, some Jews see the end of Israel's sovereignty as either inevitably necessitated by the interests of foreign nations, or as caused by melting from within. These folk are missing the understanding that Israel's sovereignty is eternal, that Israel's sovereignty is necessitated by Hashem's desire, and that Israel's sovereignty, ultimately, cannot be compromised, no matter how foolhardy secular representatives of our Holy Land act.

The flip side of this truth is that platitudes are easier to espouse than to live. Consider that a long time ago, in the Kingdom of Shushan, only "crazy" old Mordechai refused to join the banquet where the destruction of The Holy Temple was being celebrated (the Persian host, King Ahasuerus, had made an "effort" to supply his Jewish guests with "kosher" wine and meat in order to demonstrate that he had co-opted them.)

In fact, the Jews of Shushan blamed old Mordechai for the king's signing of Haman's decree to wipe us out of Ahasuerus' lands. It seems that elder Mordachi's refusal to prostrate himself to proud premier Haman had been just the excuse that the schemer, Haman, had been seeking to vanquish his resilient foe, the Jewish People (Ahasuerus never referred to his self-esteem issue.)

In the end, the Jews defeated their enemies, in general, and defeated Haman, plus his lineage, that is, his many sons, specifically (the House of Haman was hung on the gallows intended for Mordechai.) What's in between the tale's "covers," however, is stuff that's instructive for today.

Mordechai made an outlandish self-sacrifice. In essence, he gave over his wife/daughter/niece/ward (sources differ) to a king with no shortage of lascivious appetites. Although Mordachi's people lived happily ever after, Mordachi's beloved woman did not.

Furthermore, Esther, was not only forced to contend with the nastiest sorts of objectification and worse, for the rest of her life, at the hands (literally and figuratively) of an anti-Semitic king, she also had to risk her life several different times, in several different ways, to attain and to maintain that mistakenly coveted position.

As for the Jewish populous, after a lot of fasting, crying, and praying, our ancestors, Baruch Hashem, were rewarded with Heavenly Mercy; we were not exterminated. That we exist is proof enough. Yet, our forbearers could not party hardy once The Boss green-lighted our rescue.

Rather, G-d's forgiveness did not, in any form, substitute for our histadlut. Our ancestors had to mobilize and to kill the many races, which had been united under the Persian Empire, and which would otherwise have celebrated our genocide (sound familiar?)

Flash forward to the present. The bottom line is that Creation belongs to G-d and that we Jews, His people, are supposed to be the caretakers of His Holy Land. This premise, while authenticity guaranteed, is not automatically actualized. We have to work to make it real.

Consequently, it's kind of dumb to want Israelis (whether the individuals doing the wishing are locals or foreigners) to give up Israel. We can't (even though we're not always mindful of the depth of our stewardship). Much more so, we Jews can't yield our heart of hearts, Jerusalem. As for the settlements, we've no interest in cutting off our fingers and our toes just to conform to outsiders' political whims. Such behavior hurts. Such behavior is illogical. Such behavior does not tend to make The Boss happy with us, his appointees.

Per our government agencies promising one thing (e.g. recognizing the authority of the Sanhedrin), but acting on another (e.g. disregarding that court's ruling), we can understand that, sometimes, human behavior is fear-based. Fear makes people avoid actions (e.g. confronting international "partners"), freeze in the face of actions (e.g. fail to leave a government coalition that is trampling on its constituents), or mobilize. I vote for the last of these there options, for rallying.

We need leaders. While we wait for Moshiach to show us the way to directly challenge our enemies, we must follow Mordachi's example. We must refuse to participate in celebrations of our demise, and we must bring ourselves to sit at the gates of government to loudly grieve the ends to which our "leadership," in cahoots with our own inaction, is trying to take us. We must make great personal sacrifices to better insure Eretz Yisrael's well-being.

We can pray. We can trust that Hashem has not carried us this far, over the course of history, and through many kinds of suffering, only to drop us. We can pray some more.

So, feel angry when you hear that the world is against Am Yisrael and Eretz Yisrael. Thereafter, transform your anger into a calculated strategy for change. It's more than okay to address Israel's problems directly and to strip away the masks of those who try to deceive us. It's more than okay to contribute to our redemption.

Conclusion: Units of Exchange

The sun washes the sky outside of my Jerusalem window, painting the hills in streaks of gold and lavender, I breathe in the almost quiet of my salon. One child is babysitting, another is finishing trigonometry, a third is home coughing, and a fourth is exploring the wilds of a neighbor's playroom. Some of the golden streaks deepen not so much to crimson as to periwinkle, as the child with the cough rummages for a lap blanket, and as the phone vibrates. Traffic, as seen from my perch, begins to congest on the main road between Jerusalem and Tel Aviv.

In these transitional moments, I think about what my mother once said; "small children step on your feet, big ones step on your heart." I had no idea what she was talking about. In innocence, I grew up, got married, went to school, had babies, worked, and made aliyah. Decades of sunsets followed. My own babies grew up. Mom was right.

Periwinkle deepens to indigo. The last of the gold becomes gamboge and cerise. The traffic lights in the valley below become distinct. At this stage, when I "know everything," I merely need to nod to give over wisdom to my children. In the same way, when "I know nothing," no amount of kinetics can telegraph my perceptions to them. As for the gradations in between, my teens have yet to distinguish carmine from alizarin, or azure from Maya blue; they are still too young.

The sky deepens. I detect maroon, burgundy, and a bit of persimmon among the reds. I see sapphire, ultramarine, and cobalt among the blues. The children are not yet too old for extra chauffeuring, homemade soups, or hours set aside for talking. They have not yet outgrown my squishy hugs, my bits of cheerleading, or my bedtime tuck-ins.

The other day, when one son finished telling me about his hours of learning, he pulled a book to his face, secure in the knowledge that I care. Another time, on a Shabbat night, when a daughter, who had fallen asleep before our meal, awoke, she was full of dozy smiles and half-opened eyes, and I was full of the need to gently place my hands on her head to bless her. Other times, the children need only the reassurance that my cell phone is not turned to silent. One contemplates driving lessons. Another grows facial hair. One insists on following her coterie. Another insists on determining the constituency of his.

The traffic thickens. The shift from one phase of the day to the other is subtle, yet dynamic. Slate, taupe, and Payne's gray begin to replace brighter colors. Soon those shades, too, resolve to a more saturated hue. My children no longer fit in the crook of my arm, on my lap, or snuggle under a blanket next to me. I no longer remind them to stop fidgeting with their sun bonnets or to wipe their feet. Independent of my guidance, they tower beyond my height, check the ultraviolet shielding of their glasses, and mop the foyer.

My babies: speak better Hebrew than I, talk about Hesder and about marriage, and back their arguments with Rashi and Rambam. I answer them with photo albums, ancient songs, silly games, and fantastic stories. We think together, for maybe five minutes at a time, about the era when we shared mud pies and kept the company of bears with chicken pox, when we "rhymed" words like "orange," "plankton," "bulbous," and "galaxy," and when we made up stories about hedgehogs yielding spatulas.

The gray yields. Stars twinkle. The congestion on the roadway eases. My offspring no longer: pull flowers when I pull weeds, mix those leaves while I make salad, or dip their chubby fingers, feet, and random kitchen utensils into the puddles I make when cleaning up their "culinary delights." Rather, they haul, during nonshemittah years, fifty pound sacks of earth to our rooftop mirpesset, cook tasty dishes for the entire family, and help clean the toilets. They wear jewelry made from fabric and clay, listen to funky yeshuv pop, and manipulate all manners of electronic goods.

Just as Hashem, today, rolled away the light before the darkness, tomorrow, too, He will roll away the darkness before the light. The Jerusalem sky will again bloom with chiffon, papaya, saffron, mustard, amaranth, fuchsia, and magenta. In equally small measures, my children will guide their own children, will dole out the currency of Jewish parenting, giving my grandbabies the kindness, respect, silliness, grace, imperfection, and emunah that bind our generations. Such is our Israeli life.

Glossary:

\#

120 years - the span of life mentioned in Torah.

A

Achdut - unity.

Ahavat Yisrael - loving your fellow Jew.

Aliyah(ot) - act(s) of moving up; either moving to Israel, or being called up to the Torah.

Am Yisrael - The Nation of Israel (vs. the modern state).

Avodas Hashem - service to G-d.

Avot - fathers; Abraham, Isaac, and Jacob.

Ayn Tzor K'elokain - there is no artist like our G-d.

B

Bagrout - Israeli standardized subject-specific high school tests much like New York State regents.

Bar Mitzvah(Bnai Mitzvah) - when a boy comes of age, takes on responsibility or his spirituality, occurs on his thirteenth birthday.

Baruch Dayan HaEmet - Blessed is the True Judge (said upon hearing grave news).

Baruch Hashem - Bless the Name of G-d.

Bat(B'not) Bayit - daughter(s) of the house; socially adopted daughter(s).

B'ayin Tova - in a good eye/with a good outlook.

Bedecken - veiling of a bride.

Beit HaMikdash - The Temple, House of the Holiness.

Beit Knesset - synagogue, house of prayer.

Ben(Bnai) Bayit - son(s) of the house; socially adopted son(s).

Ben Yehudah - Ben Yehudah Street; a popular, pedestrian mall.

Bentshen Lecht - to recite the prayer over lighting candles on Sabbath eve or on a Holy Day eve.

B'ezrat Hashem - with G-d's help.

BH - Baruch Hashem, Bless G-d.

Bilaam - a wicked diviner.

Birkat Hamazon - Grace after Meals.

Birkat Kohanim - the Priestly Blessing.

Birkat HaShachar - morning blessings.

B'li Ayin Hara/ Kein Eina Hara - without an evil eye/with a good outlook.

B'li Nadir - without making an oath.

Bochar(im) - student(s), especially of a yeshiva.

Bracha(ot) - blessing(s).

Brit Milah - covenant of circumcision.

B'tochen - trust in G-d.

C

Challah(ot) - special braided breads eaten during the seudot of hagim and Shabbat.

Chametz - leavened products that are forbidden to be consumed on Pesach.

Charaedi - (member) of an Orthodox Jewish sect that adheres to the traditional form of Jewish law.

Charif - hot in spirit or flavor.

Chatan - bridegroom.

Chatana(ot) - wedding(s).

Chelm - city in Poland, known for Jewish stories about its allegedly naive residents.

Chesed - kindness.

Chol Hamoed, Mo'ed - the intermediate days of the Pesach and Sukkot festivals.

Chorban - sacrifice.

Chorban Pesach - Passover sacrifice.

Chovot HaLevavot - Duties of the Heart, the primary work of the Jewish philosopher Bahya ibn Paquda.

Chuppah - wedding (canopy).

City of David, The - a major archaeological site, Biblical Jerusalem.

Counting the Omer - counting the days between the festivals of Pesach and Shavu'ot.

D

Daled Amot, Four Amot - the "space" for which a person is spiritually responsible. Guests are escorted at least four amot from one's door.

Individuals are forbidden to sit or walk through another person's four amot when that person is praying the Amidah.

Daven - pray.

Drashah(ot) - scholarly interpretation(s) of religious texts.

Dvar(Dvrai) Torah - speech(es) on Torah.

E

Emunah - faith.

Eretz Yisrael - Land of Israel.

F

Fryer - socially naïve person.

G

Gan Eden - Garden of Eden.

Gemara - commentary on the *Mishna.*

Geulah - redemption.

Glatt Kosher - a strict standard of kashrut.

H

Hag(im) - holiday(s).

HaKodesh Baruchu - The Holy One, Blessed be He, G-d.

Halacha - religious laws.

Hamantaschen - filled, triangular pastry eaten during Purim.

Hanukkah HaBayit - house dedication.

Hanukkah HaClinic - clinic dedication.

Har Sinai - Mt. Sinai.

Has v'Shalom - G-d forbid.

Hasa'ah - shuttle.

Hashem - G-d.

Hashkafah(ot) - worldview(s), philosophy(ies), perspective(s).

"Hatikva" - "The Hope," Israel's national anthem.

Hesder - an Israeli *yeshiva* program combining Talmudic studies with military service.

Hillel - famous religious leader associated with the development of the *Mishnah* and the *Talmud.*

Histadlut - effort needed to make something happen, maximum effort.

Holy Land, The - Eretz Yisrael.

Hutz L'Aretz - lands outside of Israel.

I

IYH, Im Yirtzeh Hashem - if it be G-d's will.

K

Kalev ben Yefuneh - one of two spies who brought back good reports about ancient Israel.

Kallah - bride.

Kashrut - Jewish dietary laws.

Kedusha - holiness.

Kehila - community.

Kever(im) - gravesite(s), especially of sages.

Kippa(ot) - yamika(s).

Klal Yisrael, The Klal, Am Yisrael - The Nation of Israel, i.e. the people. The land is called "Eretz Yisrael."

Kohan(im) - priest(s).

Kohelet - Ecclesiastes.

Kotel - The Western Wall.

Kugel - a pudding of noodles, potatoes, or vegetables.

L

Levayah - funeral.

Lashon Hara - true, derogatory speech about another person.

M

"Machar" - "Tomorrow," a song.

Madregah(ot) - a step, elevation, or level.

Magen David - Shield of David, emblem of Judaism.

Manna - food miraculously provided for the Israelites in the wilderness during their flight from Egypt.

Mechitzah - partition to prevent the mixing of men and women.

Menorah - candelabrum used during Hanukah.

Mesilat Yesharim - an ethical text composed by Rabbi Moshe Chaim Luzzatto.

Mezuzah(ot) - parchment(s) inscribed with religious texts and attached in a case to the doorpost of a Jewish house as a sign of faith.

Minhag - custom.

Mirpesset - balcony.

Mishna - exegetical material embodying the oral tradition of Torah.

Mitzvah(ot) - deeds of loving kindness.

Mitzvot Adom l'Chaveiro - commandments governing the relationship among human beings.

Mitzvot Bein Adom l'Makom - commandments governing the relationship between us and G-d.

Modeh Ani - first words of the prayer spoken by Jews upon awakening.

Moshe Rabbeinu - Moshe, Our Teacher.

Moshgiach - trained individual who performs the task of guarding kashrut.

Moshiach - The Messiah.

Mussaf - additional prayer service recited on Shabbat, Yom Tov, Chol Hamoed, and Rosh Chodesh.

Mussar – guidelines for character development.

N

Neshemah(ot) - soul(s).

New World, The - North America.

O

Old World, The - Israel.

Oleh(im)/Olah(ot) - immigrant(s) to Israel.

Oleh Chodesh(Olim Chodeshim) - new immigrant(s) to Israel.

P

Parsha(ot) - chapter(s) (in life), weekly Torah portion.

Parve - containing no meat or milk (or their derivatives).

Payot - sidelocks.

Pesach - Passover.

R

Rabbanim - rabbis, especially yesteryear's sages.

Rambam - paramount medieval Jewish philosopher.

Rashi - medieval French rabbi, highly esteemed author of comprehensive commentary on *Talmud*.

Rav - rabbi.

Rebbe(s) - rabbi(s), Torah teacher(s).

Rosh Chodesh - new moon/month.

Ruach – divine inspiration, energy, excitement.

S

Sabra - Israeli born Jew.

Seder - Jewish ritual service and ceremonial dinner for beginning of Passover.

Sefer Tehillim - Psalms.

Seminary - a religious college that prepares Orthodox Jewish women.

Seudah(ot) - festive meal(s).

Shabbat(ot) - Sabbath(s).

Shabbat Shalom - Good Sabbath.

Shacharit - morning prayer service.

Shadchan - matchmaker.

"Shalom Aleynu" - "Peace will Come to Us," a song.

Shalom Bayit - peaceful and happy relationship between a wife and husband.

Shammai - a rabbi important to the development of *Mishna.*

Shavuot - holy day celebrating Moshe Rabbeinu receiving the Ten Commandments.

Shema - the centerpiece of morning and evening Jewish prayers.

Shemittah - one year in seven, in Israel, during which it is prohibited to treat the land as personal property; many agricultural (products) restrictions apply.

Sheva Brachot - seven blessings said after wedding feasts, which occur for seven days.

Shidduch(im) - relationship match(es), marital partnership, Jewish system of matchmaking.

Shidduchim, In/ Shidduch Parsha - span of life in which one seeks a match.

Shir Shel Yom - song/psalm of the day of the week.

Shiur - Talmudic study session.

Shoah - Holocaust.

Shofar - ram's-horn trumpet.

Shtender - a personal bookstand.

Shuk - (open air) market.

Shul - synagogue.

Siddur(im) - prayer book(s).

Simcha(Sma'achot) - celebration(s) of important life events.

Sponga - clean with a squeegee floor mop.
Sukkot - Feast of Tabernacles.

T

Tallis (im) - prayer shawls.
Talmid(im) chacham(im) - wise man(men) who is(are) always studying.
Talmud - oral law/oral Torah; consists of the *Mishna* and the *Gemara.*
Techum - Shabbat and holiday limit on travel.
Tefillah(ot) - prayer(s).
Tefillah Haderech - Travelers' Prayer.
Tehillim - Psalms.
Teshuva - repentance.
Tisch - reception.
Tzedek(et) - righteous person.
Tzedakah - charity.
Tzionite - Zionistic.
Tzitzis - specially knotted, ritual fringes found on tallisims.
Tznius - modest

V

Va'ad - council of community rabbis.

Y-Z

Yehoshua - Joshua, one of two spies who brought back good reports about
    ancient Israel.
Yeshiva - Orthodox Jewish men's college.
Yeshuv - Jewish community or settlement.
Yeshuvnik - someone living on a yeshuv.
Yetzer Hara - evil inclination.
Yetzer Tov - good inclination.
Yiddishe - Jewish.
Yiddishkeit - Judaism.
Yom Tov - a good day, a holiday.
Yoman - date book, diary.
Yomim Noraim - High Holy Days, Days of Awe, a 10-day period of
    introspection and repentance.
Zehut - merit.

Credits:

"A Bat Bayit's Aliyah" as "A Bat Bayit's Aliyah, Part I" and "A Bat Bayit's Aliyah, Part II." "Old/New World Discourse." *The Jerusalem Post*. Jan. 6 and 13, 2008.

"A Springtime Letter to Friends." "Old/New World Discourse." *The Jerusalem Post*. Apr. 15, 2007.

"Aliyah Memories." "Old/New World Discourse." *The Jerusalem Post*. Nov. 09, 2008.

"All Things Blue and Green" as "Shifting Perspective." "Old/New World Discourse." *The Jerusalem Post*. Apr. 17, 2007.

"Amidst Oranges." *Zeek*. Dec. 2009.

"An Ongoing Crisis." "Middle Eastern Musings." *The Jerusalem Post*. Dec. 26, 2012.

"Another Dumpster Fire." "Middle Eastern Musings." *The Jerusalem Post*. Jan 4, 2013.

"Apple-Scented Toilet Paper" as "Apple-Scented Toilet Paper: Jerusalem's String Bridge." "Old/New World Discourse." *The Jerusalem Post*. Feb. 28, 2008.

"Arab Men." *Social-i Magazine*. Dec. 2010.

"Brutality in the City: A Brief Response." "Old/New World Discourse." *The Jerusalem Post*. Jul. 02, 2008.

"Coming Prepared" as "*Tzedakah*, Part III: Coming Prepared." "Old/New World Discourse." *The Jerusalem Post*. Oct. 29, 2008.

"Communication Climate, Incommensurability, and Relationships" as "Communication Climate, Incommensurability, and Relationships, Part I" and "Communication Climate, Incommensurability, and Relationships, Part II." "Old/New World Discourse." *The Jerusalem Post.* Dec. 20 and 21, 2006.

"Communication Rules" as "A Bottoms-Up Approach to Communication Rules." "Old/New World Discourse." *The Jerusalem Post.* Dec. 4, 2006.

"Dissatisfaction with Synthetics." "Old/New World Discourse." *The Jerusalem Post.* Nov. 10, 2008.

"Faith." "She Said: She Said." *The Jerusalem Post.* Jun. 10, 2009.

"G-d's Help Masked as "Accidents" as "Hashem's Help Masked as 'Accidents.'" "Old/New World Discourse." *The Jerusalem Post.* Aug. 16, 2007.

"Good Home Beautiful." "She Said: She Said." *The Jerusalem Post.* Feb. 12, 2009.

"Hashem's Cool Creations." "She Said: She Said." *The Jerusalem Post.* Jun. 28, 2009.

"I Will Not Forget Thee, O Jerusalem!" "Old/New World Discourse." *The Jerusalem Post.* Mar. 17, 2008.

"Idolatry and the Mass Media." "Old/New World Discourse." *The Jerusalem Post.* Dec. 18, 2006.

"International Media Phubar: Rhetorically Guarding our Homeland" as "International Media Phubar: The Need to Rhetorically Guard our Jewish Home." "Middle Eastern Musings." *The Jerusalem Post.* Aug. 29, 2011.

Israel as a Spiritual Retreat" as "Metaphor, Part I: Socially 'Deviating' Israel" and "Metaphor, Part IV: Socially 'Deviating' Israel as A Spiritual Retreat." "Old/New World Discourse." *The Jerusalem Post.* Jun. 7 and 27, 2007.

"Israel as Gan Eden" as "Metaphor, Part V: Socially 'Deviating' Israel as Paradise." "Old/New World Discourse." *The Jerusalem Post*. Jun. 30, 2007.

"Israel as Moon Base Alpha" as "Metaphor, Part III: Socially 'Deviating' Israel as Moon Base Alpha." "Old/New World Discourse." *The Jerusalem Post*. Jun. 20, 2007.

"Israel as the Foyer to a More Excellent Chamber" as "Metaphor, Part VI: Socially 'Deviating' Israel: Conclusion." "Old/New World Discourse." *The Jerusalem Post*. Jul. 8, 2007.

"Israel as the Wild West" as "Metaphor, Part II: Socially 'Deviating' Israel: The Wild West." "Old/New World Discourse." *The Jerusalem Post*. Jun. 17, 2007.

"Judging Favorably" as "More about Judging Favorably." "Middle Eastern Musings." *The Jerusalem Post*. Dec. 17, 2012.

"Let's Not Forget the *Kedusha* of Jerusalem." "She Said: She Said." *The Jerusalem Post*. Aug. 30, 2009.

"Media Savvy: The Fires of Rhetoric" as "Who's a Jew, Part V: The Fires of Rhetoric." "Middle Eastern Musings." *The Jerusalem Post*. Jan. 12, 2011.

"Media Serpents" as "Of Media Serpents." "Middle Eastern Musings." *The Jerusalem Post*. Apr. 30, 2013.

"More about Island Living." "Old/New World Discourse." *The Jerusalem Post*. May 29, 2008.

"No Saintly Fools" as "A Little More Theory of Discourse, Part I: No Saintly Fools." "Old/New World Discourse." *The Jerusalem Post*. Nov. 11, 2008.

"Not So Exotic After All." "Old/New World Discourse." *The Jerusalem Post*. Jul. 30, 2008.

"Pain." "Middle Eastern Musings." *The Jerusalem Post*. May 7, 2013.

"Partying, Israeli Style." "Old/New World Discourse." *The Jerusalem Post*. Feb. 5, 2007.

"Rain." "Middle Eastern Musings." *The Jerusalem Post*. Jan. 8, 2013.

"Raising Children while Vetting Israeli Politics." "Middle Eastern Musings." *The Jerusalem Post*. Jan. 29, 2012.

"Royalty." "Old/New World Discourse." *The Jerusalem Post*. Jun. 5, 2008.

"Self-Actualization" as "Who's a Jew, Part VII: Self-Actualization." "Middle Eastern Musings." *The Jerusalem Post*. Feb. 4, 2011.

"Spies vs. Guides." "Middle Eastern Musings." *The Jerusalem Post*. Jun. 22, 2011.

"Street Smarts." "Middle Eastern Musings." *The Jerusalem Post*. Nov. 18, 2010.

"Striving to Do Better." "She Said: She Said." *The Jerusalem Post*. Apr. 2, 2009.

"Sweet Seudah Bar Mitzvah." "Old/New World Discourse." *The Jerusalem Post*. Mar. 28, 2008.

"Supporting the Local Economy." "Middle Eastern Musings." *The Jerusalem Post*. Feb. 12, 2013.

"That Most Important Reality Show." "Word Citizen." *The Jerusalem Post*. Sep. 18, 2017. Rpt. from "Middle Eastern Musings." *The Jerusalem Post*. Feb. 8, 2013.

"The Beauty of a Little Good." "Middle Eastern Musings." *The Jerusalem Post*. Feb. 27, 2013.

"The Cardiovascular Technologist and Others." as "Disbelief, Part III: The Cardiovascular Technologist, The Department Chairman, and The Utility Company Technician." "Old/New World Discourse." *The Jerusalem Post.* Jul. 22, 2007.

"The Challot and the Kallot." "Old/New World Discourse." *The Jerusalem Post.* May 5, 2008.

"The Holy Land." "She Said: She Said." *The Jerusalem Post.* May 27, 2009.

"The Importance of Hands on Giving" as "*Tzedakah,* Part II: The Importance of Hands on Giving." "Old/New World Discourse." *The Jerusalem Post.* Oct. 26, 2008.

"The Music." "Old/New World Discourse." *The Jerusalem Post.* Feb. 20, 2007.

"The Olive Pickers." "Middle Eastern Musings." *The Jerusalem Post.* Nov. 14, 2011.

"The Path of Torah *is* the Path of the Feminist." "Old/New World Discourse." *The Jerusalem Post.* Mar. 03, 2008.

"The Soldiers' Solution." *Splash of Red.* Jan. 2010.

"Truly Alone." "Middle Eastern Musings." *The Jerusalem Post.* Mar. 17, 2011.

"*Tzedakah*: The Magnitude of a Proper Standpoint" as "*Tzedakah* Part I: The Importance of a Proper Standpoint." "Old/New World Discourse." *The Jerusalem Post.* Oct. 19, 2008.

"Unbelievable" as "Unbelievable: Part Two: Local Lunacies." "Middle Eastern Musings." *The Jerusalem Post.* Nov. 29, 2012.

"Units of Exchange." *Mishpacha Magazine's Family First.* Feb. 20, 2008. 30. Rpt. as "Units of Exchange" in *The Best is Yet to Be.*

Miriam Liebermann. Ed. Targum. 2011. 36-38.

"Visiting the Kotel." "She Said: She Said." *The Jerusalem Post*. May 17, 2009.

"Welcome Home." "Old/New World Discourse." *The Jerusalem Post*. Aug. 22, 2007.

"Why the Sudden Interest." "Middle Eastern Musings." *The Jerusalem Post*. Mar. 4, 2011.

"Yoman, Day Planner, of a Mad Housewife" as "Yoman (Diary) of a Mad Housewife," "Old/New World Discourse." *The Jerusalem Post*. Mar. 7, 2008

Bibliography:

Alsaegh, Alaa. "Cries from the Heart of the Holocaust." *Arabs for Israel*. 27 Sept., 2011. http://arabsforisrael. blogspot.co.il/2011/09/poem-by-iraqi-poet-alaa-alsaegh.html.

Arush, Rabbi Shalom. "The Cow Comes, the Cow Goes." Trans. Rabbi Lazer Brody. *Breslev.co.il*. http://www.breslev.co.il/articlePrintVersion. aspx?id=24315&language=english.

Arush, Rabbi Shalom. *The Garden of Gratitude*. Nanuet, NY: Feldheim, 2005.105.

Bell. Larry. "Al Gore's Oil-Fueled Al Jazeera Deal Follows A String Of Green Energy Fiascos." *Forbes*. Jan 8, 2013. https://www.forbes.com/sites/larrybell/2013/01/08/al-goresoil-fueled-al-jazeera-deal-follows-a-string-of-green-energy-fiascos/#3600f881369e.

Darwish, Nonie. "Why Muslims Must Hate the Jews." *American Thinker. com*. 3 Aug., 2012. http://www.americanthinker.com/articles/2012/08/why_muslims_must_hate_jews.html.

Davidson, Ari. "Prime-Time Jihad." *Breslov.co.il*. http://www.breslev.co.il/article-PrintVersion.aspx?id=23927&language=hebrew.

Dror, Yuval. "Udderly Marvelous Gina: Israel's Most Productive Cows." *Haaretz*. https://www.haaretz.com/udderly-marvelous-gina-israels-most-productive-cow-1.123444.

Eichner, Itamar. "Is that a bomb strapped to your head? [sic]." *YNet*. 11 Nov., 2007. https://www.ynetnews.com/articles/0%2C7340%2CL-3477136%2C00.html.222

"Eliora." "A Gap-Year Student: I Took Peace for Granted." Stop the Rockets: Social Task Force for Israel. Facebook. 2012.

Franklin, Pat. "Wonders of Islam: Muslims attack Christian convert in broad daylight in St Louis and carve the Star of David on his back [sic]." The Free Press. 31 Nov., 2011. http://www.thefreepressonline.co.uk/news_print/1/2334.htm. 31 Nov., 2011.

Geller, Rabbi Yehoshua. Letter to the author. 5 Nov. 2014. TS.

Gross, Amit. et. al. "Environmental Impact and Health Risks Associated with Greywater Irrigation: A Case Study." Researchgate.net. Feb. 2005. https://www.researchgate.net/publication/7455989_Environmental_impact_and_health_risks_associated_with_greywater_irrigation A_case_study.

Hecht, Rabbi Yitzchok. "Yehoshus and Kalev." "Weekly Dvar Torah." National Council of Young Israel. 17 June, 2017. http://www.yihillcrest.org/Parsha/Shelach2017.pdf.

"Israel: The Holy Land." Chabad.org. http://www.chabad.org/library/article_cdo/aid/588018/jewish/Israel.htm.

Jacobson, Yoseph Y. "Souls in the Rain." Chabad.org. http://www.chabad.org/library/article_cdo/aid/2557/jewish/Souls-in-the-Rain.htm.

Kalmus, Jonathan. "The 'tefillin terrorist' and a New Zealand ferry [sic]." The Jewish Chronicle. 13 Dec., 2010. https://www.thejc.com/news/world/the-tefillin-terrorist-anda-scare-on-a-new-zealand-ferry-1.20008.

Kinkaid, Cliff. "Congress Fails to Act Against Gore's Terror TV Deal." American Survival News. 31 Jan., 2013. http://www.usasurvival.org/home/ck01.31.13.html#axzz4pANiq23w.

Kurtz, Howard. "Why Al Gore's Al Jazeera Deal Doesn't Seem Right." CNN.com. 7 Jan., 2013. http://edition.cnn.com/2013/01/07/opinion/kurtz-gore-al-jazeera/index.html.

Lipson, Caryn. "This is My Territory." In A Good Place: Thoughts about Life in The Holy Land. 24 July, 2011. https://bimakomtov.wordpress.com/?s=this+is+my+territory.

Loewenthal, Dr. Naftali. "Meaning and Chaos." Chabad.org. http://www.chabad.org/parshah/article_cdo/aid/43011/jewish/Meaning-and-Chaos.htm.

Marcus, Itamar and Nan Jacques Zilberdik. "EU-funded Palestinian NGO Glorifies Hijackings, Terror, and Hatred of Israel and the US." Palestinian Media Watch. 20 Dec., 2012. http://palwatch.org/main.aspx?fi=157&doc_id=8219.

Merton, Robert K. Social Theory and Social Structure. New York: Free Press, 1967.

Padowitz, Rabbi Joel. "The 7 Ushpizin Guests." Aish.com. http://www.aish.com/h/su/dits/48965711.html.

Popack, Rabbi Eli. "When Moses 'Consoled' Aaron." Chabad.org. 14 Apr., 2009. http://webcache.googleusercontent.com/search?1=cache;nUkDzmb1FScJ:www.chabad.org/blogs/blog_cdo/aid/877253/jewish/SHEMINI-When-Moses-Consoled-Aaron.htm+&c=10&hl=en&ct+clnk&gl=il.

Prero, Rabbi Yehudah. "Chanukah and Olive Oil: Lessons in Devotion." Torah.org. https://torah.org/learning/yomtov-chanukah-5756-vol2no22/.

Reuters. "Jews Wearing Tefillin Cause Alarm Aboard Airplane." The Jerusalem Post. 13 Mar., 2011. http://www.jpost.com/Jewish-World/Jewish-News/Jews-wearing-tefillincause-alarm-aboard-airplane.

Schapira, Rabbi Nathan. "The Rains of Israel." Chabad.org. http://www.chabad.org/kabbalah/article_cdo/aid/380819/jewish/The-Rains-of-Israel-102.htm.

Scratch. "Terror in School." YouTube. 28 Nov., 2012. https://www.youtube.com/watch?v=Cbdnu_R9G40.

Shapiro, Ben "Current TV Bought by Al Jazeera." Frontpagemag.com. 10 Jan., 2013.   http://www.frontpagemag.com/fpm/172939/current-tv-bought-al-jazeera-ben-shapiro.

Sharma, Dinesh. "Cultural Diffusion in the American News Media." Al-jeezera.com. 14 Jan., 2013. Http://www.aljazeera.com/indepth/opinion/2013/01/20131141115510648291.html.

Sheinbaum, Rabbi A. Leib. "Parshas Tzav." Peninim on the Torah. http//www.shemayisrael.   co.il/parsha/peninim/archives/tzav77.htm.ten Brink, Dr. Uri. "Peace and Science in the Middle East." IRIS/SSA Distinguished Lectureship. 2008. https://woodshole.er.usgs.gov/project-pages/dead_sea/.

Warner, David and Larry McShane. "Jewish teen's tefillin sets off bomb scare that diverts US Airways flight from LaGuardia Airport." [sic]. Daily News. 21 Jan, 2010. http://www.nydailynews.com/news/national/jewish-teen-tefillin-sets-bomb-scare-diverts-airways-flight-laguardia-airport-article-1.183107.

About the Authors:

KJ Hannah Greenberg used to be an academic. She earned a Ph.D. in rhetoric and specialized in communication ethics. As well, Hannah was a National Endowment for the Humanities Summer Scholar at Princeton University and a reviewer for *The American Journal of Semiotics.*

Upon moving to Israel, Hannah morphed into a creative writer. Subsequently, she was nominated four times for the Pushcart Prize in Literature and once for The Best of the Net in Literature. Among her many books are the essay collections:
Tosh: Select Trash and Bosh of Creative Writing (Crooked Cat Books, 2017)
Dreams are for Coloring Books: Midlife Marvels (Seashell Books, 2017)
Word Citizen: Uncommon Thoughts on Writing, Motherhood & Life in Jerusalem (Tailwinds Press, 2015)
Jerusalem Sunrise (Imago Press, 2015)
Oblivious to the Obvious: Wishfully Mindful Parenting (French Creek Press, 2010)
Conversations on Communication Ethics (Praeger, 1991)
Simple Gratitudes (Propertius Press, 2018, Forthcoming)

Rivka Gross née Greenberg is a full-time mother, a full-time teacher, and a full-time graduate student. In her spare time, she writes across the spectrum about both real and imagined aspects of life. Her work can be found in *The Jerusalem Post, Chabad.org, Tachlis Magazine*, and in books such as *Jerusalem Sunrise* (Imago Press, 2015).